T0123511

UNDETERRED

The Story of a Cape May Hero, Edwin J. Hill, and the Attack on Pearl Harbor

DEBORAH FRITZ

UNDETERRED
THE STORY OF A CAPE MAY HERO, EDWIN J. HILL, AND THE ATTACK ON PEARL HARBOR

iUniverse books may be ordered through booksellers or by contacting:

iUniverse
1663 Liberty Drive
Bloomington, IN 47403
www.iuniverse.com
844-349-9409

ISBN: 978-1-6632-3175-8 (sc)
ISBN: 978-1-6632-3174-1 (e)

Library of Congress Control Number: 2021923127

Print information available on the last page.

iUniverse rev. date: 03/23/2022

In memory of

David B. Hill, who passed away on April 12, 2020.
Photo courtesy of Patria Garde-Hill.

William Charles "Bill" Furey, who passed away on June 30, 2021.
Photo courtesy of Amy Hopkins Furey.

FOREWORD

Edwin Joseph Hill was undoubtedly the crown prince of the Hill family. Despite his frequent absences, he was idolized by his sisters and envied by his brothers, some of whom had significant success in the business world.

Having experienced incoming in Vietnam on nearly a daily basis for twelve months, reacting and responding in a Huey gunship in one of the least popular engagements since World War II, I can appreciate the tactical gift the Japanese planners and naval tacticians gave us by uniting our diverse, isolationist country and unleashing our vast industrial might on that infamous day in December 1941.

As numerous members of the Japanese Imperial Navy's US-educated bureaucracy well knew, our ability to mobilize, industrialize, unite, and produce, over time, would eventually guarantee Allied success. The luxury of a united USA home front has, unfortunately, not been replicated in recent decades of increased political and ideological polarization.

As the author develops in her running narrative, our greatest Pearl Harbor loss was not the sunk and heavily damaged Pacific Fleet capital ships but the combat casualties. To the experienced senior enlisted and officer communities, going to war not with the navy you want but with the navy you've got, minus a large element of experienced surface warfare old hands, makes it tough.

As history, the attack on Pearl Harbor will forever remain of interest to all who study key world events that continue to shape the present in many ways. The human tragedy of loss and grief as families come to grips with the reality of war is a constant in these pages, which blend fact with fiction to usher us into times that younger generations won't understand or recognize in these days of smartphones and social media.

War is hell, as the saying goes, and we should all remember why it is incumbent upon us all to do what we can to ensure peace in a stable world.

Commander Edwin M. Furey, USN Ret.
Office in Charge, Helicopter Light Attack
Squadron Three (HAL-3) Seawolves Det. Seven, 1968

PREFACE

One December night in 2018, I was visiting my neighbor Pat. As we sat together over steaming mugs of tea, we started to talk about her husband, David. Pat told me his uncle was a Pearl Harbor hero. I started taking notes. Pat asked me if I would write a book about David's uncle, Edwin Joseph Hill. I was honored. The idea of writing a book about a Cape May native, who happened to be among the first American casualties as a result of the Japanese attack on Pearl Harbor, intrigued me enough to agree to pursue the project.

I began researching Edwin Hill and found quite a bit of information. Pat gave me the address of Commander Edwin Furey, and I wrote to him. He responded and told me his brother William (Bill) is more of the family historian. Commander Furey sent me a blog written by William Kelly. Kelly's blog provided much information for this book. In May 2019, Pat, David, my husband, and I visited Bill and his wife, Amy, in Cape May. David and Bill had an opportunity to catch up as cousins. Bill and Amy offered us a plethora of information about Edwin Hill.

I gradually met more of the Hill family. Each one offered unique perspectives. I met Patricia Tiegan, Edwin Hill's granddaughter. Then I met Ed Hill, David and Bill's cousin, who sent me wonderful photos and additional information. Other family members who helped were James and Peter Hill, introduced to me by Emily Brown, Edwin Hill's great-great-niece.

In this book, I interwove fiction with nonfiction. Fictionalizing some aspects of Edwin's story simply gave me the liberty to embellish when I lacked actual facts to work with. I wanted to get into his state of mind before and during the battle that ultimately cost him his life in the line of duty on a day when many heroes were sadly made. Additionally, I decided to tell much of the story through Edwin's point of view, almost as if I succeeded in bringing him back for a chat over coffee at the kitchen table.

While the focus is mostly on Edwin and the story of the USS *Nevada*, the narrative does cover the key points of the attack on Pearl Harbor to put Edwin's story in the greater context of such a historic event. The story certainly is not an all-inclusive account of that infamous day; rather, it attempts to provide a picture of a hero and his ship, the USS *Nevada*.

PROLOGUE

Edwin Joseph Hill stood on the beach in Cape May, New Jersey, just as the sun was setting. The beautiful orange, yellow, and pink sunset painted the sky. He was mesmerized by the whitecaps on the sea as he watched the low surf roll in from the Atlantic. A ship in full sail was out on the horizon. Coastal schooners continued to carry bulk cargoes from quarries in the granite state of Maine down the coast and on up Delaware Bay to the City of Brotherly Love.

As he reveled in the serenity of the moment, it struck him that God was ever present. In an inkling, it occurred to him that God might have a special destiny in store for him, though he had no idea what it might be. Edwin treasured that time, almost becoming one with the water. The sea was his soul. Within the tranquility, he shared his joys, his fears, and his sad times with his God. He felt so small, yet he knew he would make a difference and help others.

Cape May flowed in his blood. Both his paternal and maternal grandparents had emigrated from Ireland and chosen that alluring shore town to settle in. His family had established their roots and grown connections there.

Edwin's reverie was broken when his younger brother David called out to him, "Hey, Eddie, let's build a sandcastle!" The five brothers—Edwin, David, John, Francis, and William—quickly joined in the construction of a mighty sandcastle. The boys built a moat and a large protective wall of packed sand in an attempt to keep the incoming tide from knocking it down. As Edwin imagined knights on horses trotting up the sand-packed drawbridge, their mother called, "Boys, time for dinner! Don't forget to wash! Now! Fried flounder—your favorite!"

* * *

Reveille sounded at 0530 on December 7, 1941, rousing Chief Boatswain Edwin Hill from his bunk aboard the USS *Nevada*. Yawning and stretching as he got out of bed and dressed for the day, he anticipated nothing more than the usual quiet Sunday. He made his way to the mess hall for chow, a hearty meal of eggs, toast, and orange juice. After he finished eating, he grabbed a cup of mess hall coffee. Then he headed up to the top deck and pulled out his binoculars. His eyes focused on the USS *Pennsylvania*, the flag ship. Chief Boatswain Hill closely watched the colors she was flying. Then he blew his boatswain's pipe.

The American flag was being hoisted, and the marine band started playing "The Star-Spangled Banner." Chief Boatswain Hill stood at attention as the colors were raised. In the distance, however, a droning sound from the southwest grew more pronounced with every passing minute. Edwin looked in that direction and cocked his neck as he strained to listen over the music.

Edwin had planned to attend Mass on the aft deck after colors, but suddenly, there was a loud rat-a-tat-tat. This was certainly not a drill! He looked up in time to see a red circle on the bottom of a Japanese Kate torpedo bomber. The pilot was visible, as he was flying so low. Chief Boatswain Hill heard the frantic voice of Ensign Joseph Taussig over the loudspeaker: "General quarters! General quarters!" This was the real thing.

Chief Boatswain Hill and Boatswain's Mate First Class Solar gathered some of the wide-eyed privates standing in shock. They were only teenagers. Chief Boatswain Hill ordered them to stand behind the turrets. He knew they were terrified. They had never seen so many planes. Chief Boatswain Hill had never seen so many planes either, and at that moment, he knew the world had forever changed—and not for the better.

CHAPTER 1

No hero springs from the soil fully developed. The spirit of patriotism and courage it takes to put your life on the line for what you believe in does not originate in a vacuum. It grows slowly, like a seedling to an oak, and eventually, the strength within the hero's soul becomes strong enough to withstand the storms of life. As we explore Edwin's life and the events that occurred on that fateful day in 1941 aboard the USS *Nevada*, it is necessary to trace Edwin's family history.

The following pages will provide a glimpse into Edwin's background, allowing you to see what shaped him into the man he became. The narrative is told from Edwin's point of view in the first person, giving the story a more immediate and intimate feel.

* * *

My father, John Joseph Hill Sr., was born in 1853 to John Martin Hill and Julia Marie Burke. Upon emigrating from Galway, Ireland, they chose to settle in the state of Pennsylvania. My family originally lived in Philadelphia. Plentiful jobs and a sizable Irish population in the city made the area appealing to them.

John Joseph Hill Sr.
Photograph courtesy of Ed Hill, from his personal collection.

Father apprenticed as a contractor and architect in Philadelphia.[1] John Sr. was not a tall man, but he was sturdy and muscular. He was handsome, with brown hair and striking blue eyes. Gracious and considerate to everyone, John Sr. was known for his kindness. However, his sharp Irish temper was known to lie just below the surface.[2]

John Hill was young when he was an apprentice to an architect and builder named Bloch. At some period, he went into a partnership with Mr. Bloch's son. Under the name of Bloch and Hill, they built houses. They did well—until Mr. Bloch's son absconded with all the firm's assets.[3]

Father arrived in Cape May in about 1879. He searched for an adequate and affordable place to stay, at least for several months. He noticed an advertisement in the newspaper for boarders, placed there by the Halpin family. After visiting the boardinghouse and receiving a tour, John Sr. made up his mind to stay there for a while. Father then became the superintendent of the construction of the New Columbia Hotel, which had burned down the year before.[4] He also rebuilt the old Saint Mary's Church and completed a number of other contracts.[5]

* * *

Cape May is the oldest seashore resort, and it is located at the southernmost part of New Jersey, where the Delaware Bay and the Atlantic Ocean meet. Victorian architecture is part of the culture of Cape May, which numbers second only to San Francisco.[6] Cape May has held the esteemed designation of national historic landmark status since 1976.[7]

Cape May Beach.
Photograph by Deborah Fritz, May 2019.

Numerous buildings were burned in the Great Fire of Cape May on November 8, 1878.[8] It broke out in the attic of the Ocean House's new wing.[9] Arson was suspected.[10] By the time the fire was contained eleven hours later, forty acres of prime real estate had been destroyed, including some of Cape May's finest hotels.[11]

The town was known as a resort location as far back as the 1830s, when the wealthy elite from Philadelphia, New York, Washington, and

Baltimore became enamored with Cape May. After Henry Clay spent two weeks in Cape May, its reputation as a major seaside retreat on the East Coast grew exponentially.[12]

* * *

The demand for my father's abilities in construction after the fire meant it would be possible for him to put permanent roots down in the sandy soil of Cape May. Father and Mother were married in 1880 at Our Lady of the Sea Church in Cape May. A stained-glass window in the church was dedicated to my mother, Helen Aloysia Halpin. They lived at Grandmother Halpin's home in Cape May at 12 Decatur Street.

Later, Father and Mother moved to 1706 Summer Street in Philadelphia. They eventually bought a house on Twenty-Third Street, between Norris and Diamond.[13] There, my siblings and I were born. My brothers and sisters, according to age, were Mary; Helen; John Jr.; William, who died in infancy; Francis; Rose; David; and William. I was born between Francis and Rose.

Helen Halpin-Hill and son William.
Photograph courtesy of Ed Hill, from his personal collection.

Father also maintained his architect's office and drafting room at that house. At times, my father, John Sr., had downtown offices, one at Fourth and Commerce Streets and another at Sixteenth and Filbert Streets in Philadelphia. When work was slack, Father worked for the Barber Asphalt Paving Company.[14]

For a considerable time, Father was job superintendent for Ballenger and Perrot, who were institutional builders of the day. Father ran large construction work in both Pennsylvania and New York.[15]

My sister Mary was born on December 19, 1885. She was the most talented of all of us. Mother arranged for voice lessons, and she went to California to work with Groucho Marx.

Mary Hill, 1965.
Photograph courtesy of David B. Hill Jr.'s personal collection.

My brother John Jr. was born on October 18, 1889. Being the firstborn son, he was named after Father. John Jr. became a brilliant businessman, beginning his career as a machinist.

John Joseph Hill Jr. being held by his father,
John Joseph Hill Sr. Photograph courtesy of Ed Hill.

Distinguishing himself as a skilled craftsman and leader, my brother John became the founder and president of the Hill-Chase Steel Company, also known as Hill Chase and Co.[16] The company was formed in February 1929 by John J. Hill Jr. and Charles H. Chase, along with several other employees of the Edgar T. Ward Steel Service Center in Philadelphia.[17] The Hill-Chase Steel Company was located on Trenton Avenue and Ontario Street in Philadelphia.

The company was known for its innovations in steel, such as when Richard T. James consulted engineers from Hill-Chase to assist him with his new invention, the Slinky, a steel-spring toy that could "walk" down steps.[18] After the Slinky was perfected, steel was purchased from the Hill-Chase Steel Company to supply inventory for mass production of the toy.[19]

Companies took notice of Hill-Chase Steel. Other clients who used the Hill-Chase Steel Company's services included Remington, Underwood, and Smith-Corona Typewriters.[20] The Hill-Chase Company also sold steel to build the railroad cars of the *Spirit of St. Louis* and the *Spirit of Los Angeles* high-speed trains.[21]

John J. Hill Jr. Photograph courtesy of
Ed Hill, from his personal collection.

My two sisters were born with business savvy like our brother John Jr. Helen was born on July 15, 1888, and Rose was born on March 28, 1895.

Helen, 1898. Photograph courtesy of Ed Hill,
from his personal collection. Photo cropped by Deborah Fritz.

My aunts on Mother's side also lived in Cape May: Aunt Kate, Aunt Rose, Aunt Mary, and Aunt Amelia. My aunts, along with my sister Rose and my brother William, owned and managed the Windsor Hotel in Cape May from the 1920s until the 1940s. The Windsor Hotel was truly grand and considered one of the flagship hotels in Cape May.[22]

Postcard of the Windsor Hotel, 1957. Property of Deborah Fritz.

My sister Rose married a reputable physician, Dr. Charles Furey. He helped to run the Windsor as well. The Windsor Hotel was revolutionary in that it had heated rooms. In this way, the hotel was able to accommodate guests year-round.

Dr. Charles Furey and Rose Hill-Furey.
Photograph courtesy of William Furey, from his personal collection.

Throughout most of the twentieth century, business was good at the Windsor, even as other hotels struggled.[23] The Windsor Hotel was purchased by the Halpin and Hill families in the early 1920s. At the hotel, we, as a family, worked, conversed, and generally spent time together. The Windsor was where we became grounded, rejuvenated, and renewed. It was my favorite place, and it brings much nostalgia as I think of it.

In addition to their commitments at the Windsor, my sisters Rose and Helen ran the nearby Congress Hall.

Postcard of Congress Hall. Date unknown.
Property of Deborah Fritz.

Congress Hall had earned a reputation as being a "glittering refuge for the wealthy."[24] The lawns of our Congress Hall hosted the country's first baseball game. The Philadelphia Athletics played against nine gentlemen vacationing at another hotel. The Athletics were victorious, though they had more competition from the gentlemen than they anticipated.[25]

Unfortunately, Congress Hall fell victim to the Great Fire in 1878. The owners were not about to chance building the hotel with flammable wood again. Within a year, Congress Hall was reconstructed out of brick.[26]

At least four US presidents stayed at Congress Hall: Franklin Pierce, James Buchanan, Ulysses Grant, and Benjamin Harrison. Partisans of

Congress Hall fondly pointed out that the hall was a kind of "Summer White House" while the real White House was being renovated in 1890–1891.[27]

Twenty-eight-year-old John Philip Sousa visited Congress Hall in 1882. There, he led the US Marine Corps Band in a weeklong concert series on the lawn of Congress Hall,[28] where he composed "Congress Hall March."

I found it humorous that our Congress Hall opened Cape May's first post-Prohibition cocktail bar in 1934.[29]

Left to right: Bill Casselman (Helen's son), Helen, William, and Rose. Photograph courtesy of Ed Hill.

Though Congress Hall was closed during World War II, Rose hosted Ann Dupont and her Rhythmen on her lawns in 1945 (after my death). Ann Dupont was known as Queen of the Clarinet, and she drew large crowds to Congress Hall.[30]

Left to right: Rose Furey, William Hill, and Helen Hill-Casselman.
Photograph courtesy of Ed Hill, from his personal collection.

My brother Francis was born on April 21, 1892. He worked as an apprentice in the same machine shop as my brother John when they were young men.

During World War I, Francis worked as a brad man for the New York Central Railroad in Cleveland, Cuyahoga County, Ohio. During World War II, he served as a private in Regular Army Second Field.

Later, a house was named after Francis Hill, located at 1001 Beach Drive in Cape May.

Francis Hill House. Photograph by Deborah Fritz, May 2019.

My youngest brother, William, was born on May 11, 1899. He was the second William. The first William Hill was born on November 16, 1889, but, tragically, died the same day.

William lived at the Windsor Hotel and worked as an assistant manager under our sister Rose. A son named Ed Hill was born to William and his wife, Rosalie. Later, William worked at W. A. Taylor and Company.[31] Eventually, William and his family moved to Miami, Florida, where he founded and owned the Hill Fan Company.

Photograph of William A. Hill, courtesy of Ed Hill.

My brother David Bernard Hill was born on August 3, 1897. His story is remarkable. Our wonderful mother passed away in 1911. Helen and Rose were unable to supervise David and me. Mary was in California. It was hard for Helen and Rose to watch us and work the hotels at the same time.

I enlisted in the US Navy at seventeen, and David followed my example. He was only fifteen years old at the time. He ran away from home because our aunts would never have allowed him to enlist at fifteen. World War I was just breaking out in Europe. The navy's minimum age requirement was eighteen; however, the navy readily recruited David, as he appeared older than he was and was physically fit.

My brother David was assigned to the ship USS *Panther,* which was docked in the Philadelphia Navy Yard. She was used to transport US troops across the Atlantic to Europe. David worked in the boiler room, shoveling coal. It was tiring and arduous work, but David was young and strong, which would serve him well in the future.

After the USS *Panther* was berthed in Brest, France, the sailors were ordered and equipped to fight with the infantry. While David's company fought in the trenches in the French countryside, he and one of his crewmates were ordered to advance and take ground. The German Army surrounded the area. David and his crewmate were hiding in some bushes. They tried to make a run for it to an old abandoned building. However, German infantry immediately spotted and captured them.[32]

When World War I ended, the British removed the survivors from the prison camps and cared for them in England. David had no recollection of how he'd ended up as a patient in Britain. When David was well enough to travel, the British health care workers arranged for him to board a ship bound for America.

When the ship arrived in Manhattan Harbor, the masters-at-arms immediately arrested him. He did not understand the charges. David was accused of leaving his post and going AWOL. He declared his innocence and explained repeatedly that he had been a prisoner of war (POW) in a German camp. The navy did not believe him and placed my brother David in the brig.[33]

Being a resourceful man, David was able to outsmart the masters-at-arms. One night, he saw an opportunity for escape from the brig and took it. David knew he could not stay in New York or anywhere on the

East Coast. David ran, hid, and hitchhiked until he reached our cousin's house in Pennsylvania. He asked our cousin to drive him to California. They ended up in Napa Valley.[34]

Photograph of David Bernard Hill, courtesy of David B. Hill Jr.'s personal collection.

One day a general was vacationing with his family in Napa Valley. David poured out his story to the general about being a POW and being accused of going AWOL. As the general listened intently to his story, he promised to bring him justice and clear his name.

The general was good for his word. When he and his family returned to New York, the general demanded a meeting with naval officials. My brother's name was officially cleared.[35] David was honorably discharged on February 12, 1925.[36]

CHAPTER 2

I, Edwin Joseph Hill, was born in October 1894.

Edwin Hill relaxing in Cape May. Photograph courtesy of William Furey, from his personal collection.

My brother William owned an amazing twenty-eight-foot racing catboat, which was kept at George Roseland's dock at Schellenger's Landing in Cape May. We used to race with friends who owned similar boats. It was great fun![1]

When I lived in Philadelphia, my first job was working at Dill and Collins. They made pulp into paper. The wood pulp transformed the industry. Before this, paper was made from cloth and linen. Philadelphia became the nation's primary papermaking center.[2]

I later moved to William's house in Cape May, but my mailing address was the Windsor Hotel.

After Mother passed, I enlisted at the US Navy recruiting station in Philadelphia on October 11, 1912. I trained to become a boatswain's mate and began active service in the US Navy on February 12, 1915. I turned twenty-one years old when I was ranked as boatswain's mate second class.[3]

Edwin J. Hill. Photograph taken in 1919 in Cape May.
Courtesy of William Furey, from his personal collection.

I would say that the boatswain's mate is the rating that most exemplifies the word *sailor.*[4] It is the oldest rating in the US Navy, established in 1797.[5] The boatswain's mate falls under the rank of chief petty officer and is a senior crewman of the deck. My responsibilities included maintaining the ship's hull: rigging, anchors, cables, sails, the deck, and small boat operations.[6]

Another name for the boatswain is *bosun* (abbreviated as *bos'n* and pronounced bō'sən). A sailor must train and demonstrate growth in experience to become an ordinary seaman (OS). After an OS gains further experience, he is promoted to the rank of able-bodied seaman (AB). When the AB has gained enough experience and possesses the necessary skills, he is promoted to boatswain's mate.[7] The subcategories under the rank of boatswain's mate (BM) are BM third class, BM second class, BM first class, and chief boatswain's mate.[8]

I acted as a watchman of the ship, both for the captain and for the superior officers. I was the liaison between the captain and the crew. Another one of my responsibilities was to ensure the ship was sea ready at all times. I was also required to have technical knowledge of pinpointing a ship's geographic position and the ability to navigate it.[9]

The first ship I was assigned to was the USS *Dixie.* I served on her from June 12, 1912, until August 8, 1915. I was proudly warranted on October 11, 1915. Promotion to a commissioned warrant officer is by selection of a statutory board, following no less than six years of warrant service.[10] US Navy regulations state that a warrant officer may succeed to command of a ship or other command of the naval service, provided he is authorized.[11] Just prior to World War II, there were eight warrant specialties: boatswain, gunner, carpenter, electrician, radio electrician, machinist, pharmacist, and pay clerk.

My next assignment was on the destroyer tender USS *Melville.* I served on her from April 6, 1917, until November 3, 1918.[12] Then I was assigned boatswain's mate second class and was soon promoted to boatswain's mate first class. At the time of my discharge after World War I on November 3, 1918, my rating was chief boatswain's mate.[13]

Photograph of Chief Warrant Officer Edwin J. Hill, courtesy of William Furey, from his personal collection.

One of the constant problems with naval ships is the corrosive properties of the salt water. As boatswain, I had to perform daily inspections on all areas of the ship. Depending upon my assessment, I would assign duties to the deck crew, such as cleaning and painting the deck. I was responsible for implementing a preventative maintenance program to ensure the ship and deck equipment were up to standards. When we had time, I enjoyed training the deck crew on damage control.[14]

The boatswain carries a special pipe, or whistle, which is approximately six inches long. The pipe consists of a narrow tube, the gun, which directs air over a metal sphere with a hole in the top.[15] The player opens and closes his hand over the hole to change the pitch. The rest of the pipe consists of a keel, a flat piece of metal beneath the gun that holds the pipe together, and the shackle, a key ring that connects a long silver or brass chain that sits around the collar. The shackle is used when in ceremonial uniform.[16]

I was one of only thirty holders of the rank of chief boatswain in the US Navy. I was commissioned to the post only three years after I enlisted.[17]

A US Navy chief petty officer's rate emblem is symbolized by crossed anchors with the letters *USN* centered on the anchor. Officially, the letters stand for "United States Navy." According to naval tradition, the letters are symbolic of the following:

> Unity: To symbolize "cooperation, maintaining harmony and continuity of purpose and action."
>
> Service: To symbolize service "to our God, our fellow man and our Navy."
>
> Navigation: "To keep ourselves on a true course so that we may walk upright before God and man in our transactions with all mankind, but especially with our fellow Chiefs."[18]

I next served under Admiral William Sims on the battleship USS *Pennsylvania* (BB-38).[19] The USS *Pennsylvania* (BB-38) was authorized by Congress on August 22 1912 and commissioned for service on June 12, 1916. She was built by the Newport News Shipbuilding and Drydock Company in Virginia.[20]

In addition, the USS *Pennsylvania* was the lead ship in her class, with the other ship being the USS *Arizona*. The USS *Pennsylvania* was one of two oil-burning ships. The other ship was the USS *Nevada*. In World War I, the Allied forces used only coal-burning ships to fight the German

Navy, as there were not enough oil tankers to send to the British Isles.[21] Instead, the *Pennsylvania* remained in American waters and took part in training exercises. In 1918, she escorted President Woodrow Wilson aboard the SS *George Washington* for the Paris Peace Conference.[22]

In 1921, the *Pennsylvania* became the flagship of the battle fleet and led the fleet for the next eight years on patrols through the Atlantic, the Caribbean, and the Pacific. From 1929 to 1931, the USS *Pennsylvania* was stationed at the Philadelphia Navy Yard while she underwent modernization. Like the USS *Nevada,* the USS *Pennsylvania's* cage masts were replaced with tripod masts. Her combat systems were modified and improved as well.[23] During World War II, the USS *Pennsylvania* participated in every major naval offensive in the Pacific. She earned eight battle stars and the US Navy Commendation Award for service.[24]

Chief Warrant Officer Edwin J. Hill standing (left front) at attention during an inspection on the USS *Pennsylvania.* Photo courtesy of Peter Hill, from his personal collection.

While I was serving on the USS *Pennsylvania* in 1920, we stopped in the Irish port of Cork. One night, there was a party in town. Some of my friends invited me to come, as we were granted leave for the evening. I made sure my shoes were polished and every button was in place.

During the party, I was kind of bored, so I walked outside to a pedestrian bridge spanning the River Lee. I noticed a beautiful woman standing on the bridge. I knew immediately she was the woman I was going to marry.

I spoke with the woman and found out her name was Catherine. She told me she worked as a milliner. We talked for a long time. After that, Catherine and I saw each other every time I could get shore leave. Things moved fast, and I proposed to Catherine. She said yes! We spoke with her parents, and the plan was for her to come to America.

Catherine Caughlin. Date unknown. Courtesy of Catherine Helen Roggeveen O'Connell, from her personal collection.

Catherine Caughlin boarded the ship RMS *Saxonia* in Tillbury, England, directly after I departed for America on the USS *Pennsylvania*. The *Saxonia* arrived in New York and then sailed to Camden, New Jersey. Catherine arrived on October 12, 1920. I was waiting for her.

I took my bride-to-be directly to Cape May. We were married on October 28, 1920, at Our Lady Star of the Sea Church, the same church where my parents were married. The ceremony was performed by Reverend E. P. Kennedy, and the reception that followed took place at the Windsor Hotel.[25] I was twenty-six at the time, and Catherine was twenty-two.[26]

Photograph by Deborah Fritz, May 2019.

Inside Our Lady Star of the Sea Church.
Photograph by Deborah Fritz, May 2019.

Certificate of Marriage

OUR LADY STAR OF THE SEA CHURCH
525 WASHINGTON STREET
CAPE MAY, NJ 08204

This is to Certify

That Edwin J. Hill

and Catherine Coughlan

were lawfully **Married**

on the 28 day of October 1920

According to the Rite of the Roman Catholic Church and in conformity with the laws of the

State of New Jersey

Rev. E. P. Kennedy

officiating in the presence of William Hill

and Rose Hill Witnesses, as appears from the Marriage Register of this Church.

Dated October 4, 2019 Fr. Mathias

Pastor

Marriage certificate of Edwin Joseph Hill and Catherine Josephine Coughlin, October 28, 1920. Courtesy of Patricia Tiegen, from her personal collection.

When Edwin and Catherine went to church, everyone could not help but stare at the stunning couple, especially with Edwin's uniform, per conversation with Patria Garde-Hill, September 2020. Original art by Deborah L. Fritz.

We were very much in love. Catherine and I had a tough time at first. Being on duty, I could not support Catherine emotionally like I wanted to. We lost a set of twins close to term. That experience was heart-wrenching. We rejoiced when our first daughter was born on September 14, 1922. She was christened Catherine after her mother. Our next baby was a boy. He was born on July 15, 1926. We named him Edwin after me. On December 24, 1929, our daughter Mary Helen Hill was born. Mary Helen died tragically at the age of four. Our hearts were broken. Our last son, Michael, was born on November 22, 1934.[27]

Catherine with unknown child. Photo courtesy of
Catherine Helen Roggeveen O'Connell,
from her personal collection.

During the years of 1931–1932, I served on the aircraft carrier USS *Saratoga*. The USS *Saratoga* (CV-3) was a Lexington-class aircraft carrier and was the fifth US Navy ship named after the 1777 Battle of Saratoga.[28] Given the original hull number of CC-3, the USS *Saratoga* was laid down on September 25, 1920, by the New York Shipbuilding Corporation in Camden, New Jersey.[29]

Originally designed as a battlecruiser, the *Saratoga* was converted into one of the navy's first aircraft carriers. She entered service in 1928 and was assigned to the Pacific Fleet for her entire career. The USS *Saratoga* and her sister ship, the USS *Lexington,* were used to develop and refine carrier tactics in a series of annual exercises before World War II.[30] Growing in experience and wisdom throughout my time in the navy, I served on other ships: the USS *Yorktown* (PG-1), the USS *Reina Mercedes*

(IX-25), and the USS *New Mexico* (BB-40). My next position was teaching at the US Naval Academy. I worked as a seamanship instructor there from 1932 to 1937.[31]

Everyone was starting to feel tension building up between Japan and the United States in the 1930s.[32] At that time, Japan conquered Manchuria and began a long and ultimately unsuccessful campaign to conquer China. The United States and China were allies, which put us at odds with the imperial interests of Japan. In July 1939, the United States announced the termination of the 1911 Treaty of Commerce and Navigation with Japan, thereby depriving Japan of oil needed to fuel its industries and war machine.[33]

In response, Japan seized oil-rich territories in Southeast Asia. In 1940, Japan entered into an alliance with Nazi Germany and Italy. In 1941, the United States severed all commercial and financial relations with Japan, which occupied all of Indochina by that time. Obviously, the situation indicated a spiral toward total world war, and people in sophisticated political circles in both parties understood that the United States would be unable to stand idly by while the rest of the globe went up in flames. Still, like ostriches, the powers in the bastions of Congress and the White House remained mired in the false notion that one could overlook evil without suffering any significant consequences.

I was to be stationed in Pearl Harbor, serving as a boatswain's mate aboard the battleship USS *Nevada*. Our family moved to Long Beach, California. My cousin drove the family out to Long Beach, where a large naval community was located. I was assigned the arduous task of floating a huge dry dock from New Orleans to the Pacific Coast, one of my most challenging missions, before taking up my post aboard the USS *Nevada*. We purchased a nice house in Long Beach, and the kids got settled in their schools. We lived in Long Beach while I was at sea. When I had shore duty, my family and I returned to Cape May when it was practical to do so. However, life was busy, and time passed quickly. We didn't get back to Cape May as often as I would have liked.

As busy as we all were at the time, the international tensions abroad weighed on me like a heavy cloak. I couldn't stop thinking about what might happen in the near future. Being in the military, I was sensitive to how the wars on both sides of the world were progressing badly, and I was keenly aware that the United States could get sucked into the conflicts in Europe and Asia with potentially dire consequences.

A letter written in October 1941 indicates just how uneasy I felt. Yet I was spending more and more time in Honolulu, carrying out my duties aboard the USS *Nevada*. Despite my uneasiness, I considered moving my wife and kids to Hawaii so I could be with them. In retrospect, I'm glad I didn't.

At Sea

October 19, 1941

Dear Aunt Mary, Rose, and Family:-

Another summer has come and gone and you are perhaps having a little rest from your arduous duties during a long hot summer.

While my letters to you have been few and far between, yet you all have been in my mind on many occasions.

Hope that you had a full house during the season and that it was profitable.

Cape May, like many another place is probably feeling the effects of the preparedness effort—perhaps the increase may justify keeping the hotel open the year round.

How are you all and what are you doing? Can imagine how the boys are growing big and strong and I know that you have your hands full.

How is Aunt Mary getting along—I hope that she is spared to us for many a day to come.

Suppose Doctor is as busy as ever and that he is his usual jovial self.

After an absence of six months from home I had ten nice days with my family, they were all well and getting along nicely, little Michael is showing marked improvement.

His heart is much better and we have hopes of his growing out of his condition.

The children are all in school and Catherine wrote that our house is a busy place in the mornings, each have a different time for school.

Some time ago I toyed with the problem of bringing my family out here where I could visit them more often, the problem is quite complicated because of schools, lack of reasonable housing and of course the expense—and then too, they are established, comfortable, and have their friends in Long Beach, so the idea of having them come out to Honolulu died a natural death.

We have been and expect to be real busy—the international situation looks bad and appears to be getting better no faster.

The Russians are slowly but surely being forced back and their chances for even a stalemate are remote, they are not receiving any real help from England or the US.

Japan, like a vulture, is awaiting her chance to pick the bones of Russian in Asia—she may find that she has another China on her hands, or even worse.

Another six months should find us tooled up to produce weapons in large quantities—barring strikes of course.

My personal opinion is that Germany must be beaten on the continent and we—plus some English, are the only ones who can do it—it will be costly, but if our way of life is worth saving we must be prepared to make the sacrifice—the war being fought on foreign soil will prevent our cities and civilian population from being despoiled—it's all a horrible thought, isn't it? ...

Your Loving Brother
Ed[34]

Naval authorities thought that keeping all the ships together at Pearl Harbor would be safe. Others saw the potential risks of keeping all the ships in one place, in case of an attack. The entrance canal to the harbor was not large, so it was possible all the ships could become bottled up. However, the prevalent thinking was that Pearl Harbor was the best place for our Pacific Fleet.

I wondered about the ships being in one place. What if the Japanese did attack? I did not want my family anywhere near the West Coast, much less in Hawaii, regardless of how much I missed them. I asked Catherine to take the kids out of school for at least a month or so until the intentions of the Japanese were clearer. One of our cousins in Cape May drove out to Long Beach and picked up my family. They drove back to Cape May and stayed at the Windsor. I felt much safer with them there.

CHAPTER 3

At times, it's important to put things into historical context. That is the case with background on both the USS *Nevada* and Pearl Harbor. Let's start with the ship.

The USS *Nevada* (BB-36) was the first superdreadnought, the largest and most powerful battleship in the fleet.[1] However, as war broke out between the United States and Japan, the vessel held the dubious distinction of being the oldest battleship to serve during the war.[2]

At any rate, authorization to build the ship passed in Congress on January 22, 1911.[3] She was the most modern of her class, with engines that burned oil for fuel, enabling her to carry the latest type of fourteen-inch batteries.[4] On November 4, 1912, the USS *Nevada*'s keel, the backbone of the battleship, was laid at the Quincy, Massachusetts, shipyards of the Fore River Shipbuilding Company.[5] By July 1914, *Nevada*'s hull had been completed, and she was ready for launching on July 11.[6] Governor Tasker Oddie of the state of Nevada; Josephus Daniels, secretary of the navy; and Franklin D. Roosevelt, assistant secretary of the navy at the time, were in attendance for the ceremony.[7] Miss Eleanor Anne Siebert, eleven-year-old niece of Governor Oddie, smashed a bottle of champagne against the prow of the ship.[8]

After her commissioning, the USS *Nevada* (BB-36) was taken to the docks for completion. There she had four turrets installed, with the number-one and number-four turrets encasing three fourteen-inch guns each.[9] Turrets two and three each held two of the big guns. In addition, some twenty-one five-inch guns were installed.[10]

The USS *Nevada*'s armor was a marked advance in both quantity and quality over that of the previous battleships.[11] The ship averaged a speed of 20.54 knots in sea trials held in Massachusetts Bay.[12]

The USS *Nevada* was the lead ship in her class, with the other ship being the USS *Oklahoma*.[13] These ships were built with the thickest possible armor protecting vital areas. The belt of armor was 13.5 inches thick and extended 400 feet along the hull.[14] However, *Nevada*'s bow and stern were not armored.

When the US Navy assigned *Nevada* the hull number of battleship BB-36, the number coincidently coincided with Nevada being the thirty-sixth state admitted to the Union.[15]

On March 11, 1916, at the US Navy Yard in Boston, Massachusetts, the USS *Nevada* was officially commissioned under the command of Captain R. D. Hasbrouck, USN.[16] On March 24, she was anchored off Staten Island, New York.[17]

Early in 1917, the USS *Nevada* sailed to Caribbean waters for spring maneuvers.[18] On February 3, 1917, word was received that the United States had broken off diplomatic relations with Germany.[19] Then, on April 6, 1917, the United States declared war on Germany.[20]

In the fall of 1917, it was learned that the USS *Nevada* would not be sent abroad to join the British Grand Fleet during World War I.[21] Though she was America's largest and best battleship at the time, the *Nevada* was built to be an oil-burning ship.[22] Oil was scarce in England. While the bulk of the US Navy's battleships sailed to England, the USS *Nevada* remained home as a training ship. Later that year, she entered the US Navy Yard in Portsmouth, Virginia, for a thorough overhaul.[23]

Original photograph of the USS *Nevada*, courtesy of William Furey, from his personal collection.

Between 1927 and 1929, most of America's battleships were modernized. The cage masts were replaced by two enormous tripod masts with three-level mast tops.[24] This was the case with the USS *Nevada*. The secondary armament was raised one deck, while the torpedo tubes were removed.[25] Eight new boilers were installed in place of only one, making the ships more powerful. Antitorpedo bulges were placed to enhance underwater protection.[26]

Obviously, the battleships in the Pacific Fleet packed a lot of firepower, but the old way of fighting naval wars was over, although that wasn't clear yet. It soon would be. Air power marked the future of warfare, as would prove to be the case in early December 1941 and throughout the rest of the continuing world war.

* * *

The beauty of Pearl Harbor is difficult to describe. Verdant green hills break up the cityscape, and the water shimmers a turquoise blue. Fluffy fair-weather cumulus clouds stud a brilliant blue sky. White sand beaches stretch out into the surf on the ocean sides of Oahu.

As idyllic as it might sound, Pearl Harbor was not all tropical paradise—far from it. The harbor served as a naval base for the Pacific Fleet. The native Hawaiians originally called the Pearl Harbor area Wai Momi,[27] meaning "Water of Pearl." Another name for Pearl Harbor was Pu'uloa, or "Long Hill."[28] To the Hawaiians, Pearl Harbor was the home of the shark goddess, Ka'ahupahau, and her brother (or son) Kahi'uka.[29] They were said to live in a cave at the entrance to Pearl Harbor. They guarded the waters against man-eating sharks.[30]

Ancient stories of the Hawaiian legends also tell of how Pearl Harbor was formed by Chief Keaunui of Ewa.[31] The chief opened the area by making it both wider and deeper, thus creating the lagoon.[32]

Ka'ahupahau resided in caves in the West Loch, while Kahi'uka lived in a cave near Ford Island. Together they warded off sharks that attempted to eat the people. Some stories say that when Ka'ahupahau and Kahi'uka saw the Wai Momi being damaged by humans in the nineteenth century, they left the area. When they left, they took the abundance of oysters that had given the harbor its name.[33] Ka'ahupahau was said to have been born of human parentage, but she transformed into a shark. These gods were friendly toward humans. It was said the people of Ewa, whom they protected, would keep the gods' backs scraped clean of barnacles. The ancient Hawaiian people depended on Ka'ahupahau to protect the harbor's abundant fishponds from intruders.[34]

The first documented European visitor was Captain James Cook in the 1770s.[35] The US government dispatched Lieutenant General John Schofield to Hawaii in 1872.[36] He was to assess Oahu's strategic value. Mr. Schofield recognized the potential of the Pearl Harbor area.[37] He recommended the United States negotiate with the Hawaiian Kingdom for use of Pearl Harbor.[38] The area was acquired as part of a reciprocity treaty between the United States and the Hawaiian Kingdom in 1875.[39] The treaty followed the government's convention held on December 6, 1884 but was ratified in 1887.[40] The United States then obtained exclusive rights to Pearl Harbor as part of the agreement. This allowed Hawaiian sugar to enter the United States duty-free.[41]

Coaling was done in Honolulu until 1900. In that year, two piers were constructed, and the first dredging of Pearl Harbor began.[42] In 1901, the United States began purchasing lands around the harbor under eminent domain.[43] Several collapses of dry dock construction were attributed to "seismic disturbances." The native Hawaiians were certain that Ka'ahupahau, the shark goddess, was angry.[44] A kahuna was summoned to appease Ka'ahupanhau.[45] Finally, after years of construction problems, the dry dock was opened in August 1919.[46]

Although the islands were of strategic value, Hawaii was merely a territory of the United States, as the island of Puerto Rico and the unincorporated territory of Midway would be later on. In 1959, Hawaii officially became a state. As history shows, Japan was quick to notice how vulnerable we were in terms of battle readiness. Admiral Isoroku Yamamoto determined an attack on Pearl Harbor was achievable.[47] The Japanese had been developing technologically advanced aircraft that were able to fire aerial torpedoes.[48] Japanese scientists developed special torpedoes with fins that enabled them to be dropped into the shallow harbor water. Admiral Yamamoto's strategy consisted of meticulous preparation and utmost secrecy. He planned to utilize aircraft carriers and planes on an unprecedented scale.[49] The Japanese pilots had begun specialized training for the Pearl Harbor attack in the spring of 1941.

In October 1941, the Japanese naval staff gave the final approval to Admiral Yamamoto's plan to deploy six heavy aircraft carriers.[50] These were to be accompanied by twenty-four supporting vessels. In addition, mini submarines would be dispatched in order to sink any warships that escaped the Japanese carrier force.[51] Japanese aircraft carriers chosen for the assault on Oahu were the *Akagi, Kaga, Soryu, Hiryu, Shokaku,* and *Zuikaku.*[52] Each aircraft carrier could transport 420 planes. Battleships, cruisers, and destroyers were also included in the force. Tankers sailed in order to fuel the ships during their passage across the Pacific.

On November 22, 1941, Admiral Isoroku Yamamoto ordered the meeting of the Imperial Japanese Naval Strike Force on Iturup Island of the South Kurils.[53] The area was chosen because of its constant fog coverage and sparse population, which offered protection for the force.

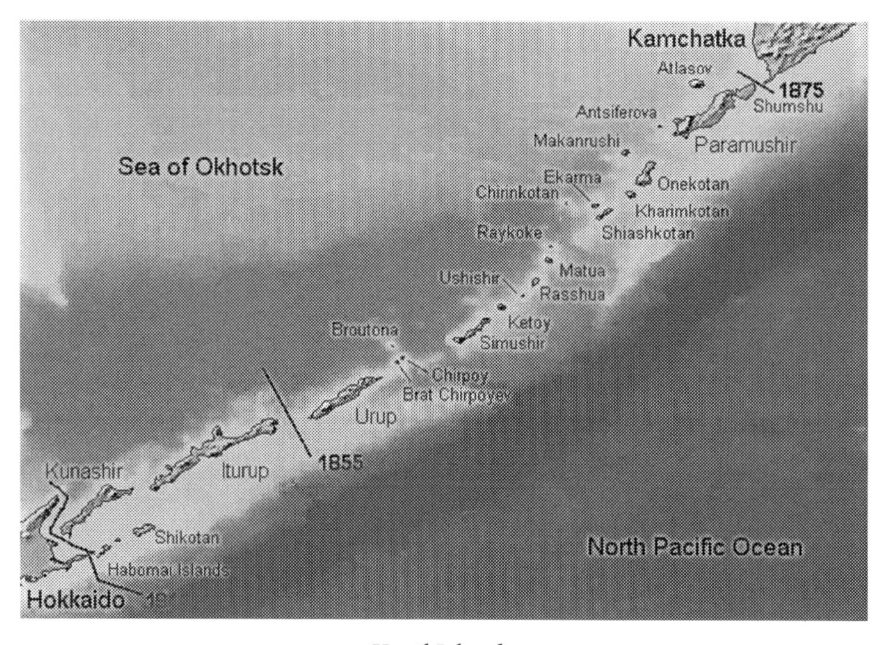

Kuril Islands

In utmost secrecy, the Hawaii Operation Strike Force left the Kurile Islands in northern Japan on November 26, 1941.[54] The force traveled for ten days across the northern Pacific through heavy seas and bad weather and under strict radio silence to avoid detection.[55] They avoided normal shipping lanes. The mission would be immediately aborted in the event they were discovered. Shortly after the Hawaii Operation Strike Force left the Kurile Islands, the Southern Operation Strike Force left for the Philippines and Southeast Asia.[56]

An advance expeditionary force of large submarines was sent to scout between Oahu, Kauai, and Molokai. Five of them were carrying mini submarines.[57] A Philippine merchant ship arrived in Nahu on Okinawa on November 30.[58] The Japanese sealed the ship's radio, and her departure was delayed in order to prevent notice of the Imperial Navy's activities.[59]

The Hawaii Operation Strike Force approached a point approximately two hundred miles north of Oahu.[60] In Japan, it was December 8, due to the nineteen-hour time difference from Hawaii.[61] The US code breakers deciphered a message from Tokyo to the Japanese embassy in Washington that ordered negotiations with the United States to be broken off at 1300 EST (0700 Hawaiian time).[62] This move was considered one step short of declaring war.

At that time, the USS *Nevada*'s hull was painted black up to her superstructure. Then her superstructure was painted white. The crew painted her various colors according to the captain's orders, but black and white were her colors during the day of the attack.

The ships of Battleship Division One—the USS *Arizona,* USS *Pennsylvania,* and USS *Nevada*—entered Pearl Harbor on Friday, December 5, 1941.[63] The crews had all been at sea, training, for two weeks. The USS *Nevada* was moored at the northeast end of Ford Island to Quay Number 8. None of the battleships were sailing that weekend because it was Vice Admiral Pye's turn to rest in port.[64]

The USS *Nevada* was not in her normal berthing place on December 7.[65] During previous fleet maneuvers, the ship had been delayed in coming into port, so the USS *Arizona* was in the vessel's usual berth, and we were in the *Arizona*'s usual berth.[66]

The US Navy's three aircraft carriers—the USS *Enterprise,* USS *Lexington,* and USS *Saratoga*—were not in port during that weekend. The USS *Enterprise* had departed Pearl Harbor for Wake Island on Friday, November 28.[67] She was delivering marine fighter aircraft. The *Enterprise* was to return to Pearl Harbor on December 6; however, bad weather delayed her.[68] Meanwhile, the USS *Lexington* departed Pearl Harbor on December 5 to deliver marine dive-bombers to Midway Island.[69] On December 7, the USS *Saratoga* was just entering San Diego from Bremerton, Washington.[70] She was carrying US Marine Corps aircraft intended for Wake Island.[71] The USS *Saratoga* got underway from San Diego, but she did not reach Hawaii until December 15.[72]

Admiral Kimmel wanted to keep his fleet concentrated in the case of any eventuality.[73] Approximately one hundred ships were in Pearl Harbor on the morning of December 7.[74] Seven battleships were moored on the eastern side of Ford Island within Pearl Harbor: *California, Oklahoma, Maryland, West Virginia, Tennessee, Arizona,* and *Nevada.*[75] The training and gunning-practice ship *Utah* was moored on the other side of Ford Island. The *Pennsylvania* was in dry dock.[76]

The navy found out in later intelligence that the Japanese planned to target Pearl Harbor's airfields first.[77] Their object was to cripple American planes while they were on the ground. This would enable the Japanese aircraft to pull off their attack without opposition. Sadly, the Japanese did a great job in carrying out their infamous sneak attack. We were caught flat-footed, and we paid dearly for our complacency.

CHAPTER 4

THE SEQUENCE OF EVENTS THAT OCCURRED SIMULTANEOUSLY ON and around Oahu on the fatal morning of December 7, 1941, are well known. Hundreds of books have been written about the carnage that took place. Yet it is still important to recap here to help put the heroic exploits of *Nevada*'s crew in perspective. The following is a timeline of key events.

0100
The Japanese launched five midget submarines ten miles off the entrance to Pearl Harbor.[1]

0350
Both the officer on deck and the quartermaster of the coastal minesweeper USCG *Condor* sighted the periscope of a submerged submarine.[2] At that time, the USCG *Condor* was located a little less than two miles southwest of the Pearl Harbor entrance buoys.[3] No submarines were supposed to be in that area at that time.[4] The *Condor* used a blinker light

to alert the patrolling destroyer USS *Ward* (DD-139).[5] After two hours of searching, the commander of the *Ward* spotted the sub headed toward the antisubmarine net at the harbor entrance.[6]

0530

Reveille sounded over the USS *Nevada*'s intercom.

The Japanese Imperial Navy strike group had gathered 275 miles north of Oahu under the shroud of rain and fog. Admiral Nagumo turned his six carriers east into the wind and increased their speed to twenty-four knots.[7]

A fleet of Japanese submarines were also headed toward Pearl Harbor. Their purpose was to torpedo any US ship that attempted to escape from the harbor into the open seas.[8] The Japanese cruiser *Chikuma* launched two E13A1 Jake seaplanes to confirm the location of the American fleet. Two hours later, they reported that the fleet was in Pearl Harbor.[9]

0545

Commander Mitsuo Fuchida led the first wave of 353 aircraft. The bombers were outfitted with telegraphs rather than microphones, so he chose Morse-style signals: *to* (..”..) and *ra* (...). *To* was to signal the attack, and *to ra* was to indicate the attack was a surprise.[10] The message was tapped three times to make sure it was received.

0630

Officials in Washington sent a message to the forces in Hawaii, alerting them about a Japanese-issued ultimatum.[11] However, as a result of atmospheric static, the message did not arrive in Hawaii until 0730.[12] Once it did arrive, the message was treated as an ordinary telegram and delivered by a motorcycle messenger on his daily rounds.[13] By 1145, the message was finally delivered to the commanding general's office almost four hours after the attack began. He did not read it until 1500.[14]

Japanese Lieutenant Haruo Yoshino wondered why Pearl Harbor was not prepared if war had been declared.[15] The Japanese military lived by the code of the Bushido of the Samurai,[16] a time-honored tradition that states if enemies are to be attacked, they should be warned first.[17] This was considered honorable. All military, especially the officers, believed this. The Japanese informed the United States of the Japanese declaration of war at least one hour before the attack.[18]

Chow call sounded on the USS *Nevada*. The sailors aboard the USS *Nevada* marched in formation for breakfast.

0637

The USS *Ward* sighted and located the periscope of the unidentified submarine originally spotted by the crew on the USGC *Condor.*[19] According to one of the action reports by Commander in Chief Pacific Fleet Headquarters, the USCG *Condor* used visual signals to notify the destroyer USS *Ward* (DD-139), which was patrolling off the Pearl Harbor entrance.[20] The destroyer sighted a periscope of an unidentified submarine trailing the USS *Antares* (AK-53) into Pearl Harbor.[21] The first shot fired by the USS *Ward* was too high, but the second struck the sub at the waterline. The sub sank, and the destroyer finished her by dropping depth charges.[22] A black oil slick spotted three hundred yards away confirmed the enemy sub had been eradicated.[23]

0645

An officer on board the *Ward* sent a verbal dispatch to the commandant of the Fourteenth Naval District.[24] It was reported received at 0712 and was subsequently transcribed.[25] Since no prior report of either contact had been made to Commander in Chief Pacific Fleet Headquarters, the report was treated like the many reports of submarine contacts from the preceding twelve months, none of which were ever confirmed.[26]

0700

US code breakers deciphered a message from Tokyo to the Japanese embassy in Washington ordering negotiations with the United States be broken off at 1300 (0730 Hawaii-Aleutian standard time).[27]

Admiral Husband Kimmel was still in his quarters, dressing and awaiting confirmation of the USS *Ward*'s report of the submarine being sunk, when Commander Fuchida's first aerial wave deployed a few miles north of Opana Station.[28]

The Japanese aircraft carrier *Akagi*'s First VT Squadron, consisting of twelve Nakajima B5N Kate torpedo bombers, turned from the southeast and assumed attack positions.[29] Behind the *Akagi*'s squadron, twelve additional Kates from the carrier *Kaga* followed. Sixteen more Kates from carriers *Hiryu* and *Soryu* came in from the southwest toward the west side of Ford Island.[30] Each Kate carried one 1,870-pound Type 91 torpedo modified to run in the shallow water of Pearl Harbor.[31] The torpedoes were also fitted with two warheads each in order to penetrate the armor belts on the battleships.

0702

Army privates Joseph Lockard and George Elliot were just finishing their 0400–0700 shift.[32] They were manning an experimental radar picket station on Opana Point.[33] Private Lockard noted a large blip on the radar screen. He thought the equipment was faulty at first, but after studying the blip closely, Private Lockard concluded it was a massive formation of planes approaching Oahu 132 miles to the north.[32] The privates called in their observation to Lieutenant Kermit Tyler at the Fighter Control Center in Fort Shafter.[34]

Lieutenant Kermit Tyler told the privates to forget it, and he did not pass the report on to higher command.[35] Even still, Private Lockard and Private Elliot surmised that the blip they saw was an unusually large number of planes.[36] The United States had five radar stations in Hawaii, and the others reported echoes more than a hundred miles offshore.

Essentially, all warnings were dismissed.

0712

When Admiral Claude C. Bloch received the news, he ordered the destroyer USS *Monaghan* to sea and ordered the harbor's antisubmarine net to be closed.[37] Admiral Bloch also called Commander Vincent R. Murphy, the Pacific Fleet commander in chief and Admiral Husband Edward Kimmel's duty officer. Admiral Kimmel was the commander in chief.[38] Commander Murphy then spent a frustrating half hour trying to get through to Admiral Kimmel's home.[39] Unfortunately, there was a language barrier with the navy operator on duty, so he was unable to understand what was being asked of him.[40]

0732

An American patrol plane sank a Japanese submarine south of the entrance buoy.[41]

0740

Another telephone call came into Commander in Chief Pacific Fleet Headquarters from the operations officer of Patrol Wing Two regarding the sub being sunk by a patrol plane.[42] Almost immediately, another telephone report came in about USS *Ward* towing a sampan—a flat-bottomed wooden vessel—into Honolulu.[43]

At a point roughly opposite Haleiwa Field, Commander Mitsuo Fuchida signaled for the general attack at 0750.[44] Each torpedo group attacked in formations of two and three. Every torpedo pilot had explicit instructions to close in on his target at the risk of his life.[45]

Commander Mitsuo Fuchida led his unit in an unplanned westerly direction along Oahu's north shore due to clouds over the Ko'olau mountain range.[46] This allowed his forces to switch to the Surprise formation.[47] He shot a single black-dragon flare to signal that the attack sequence would be Surprise.[48] In the Surprise sequence, the torpedo planes were to attack Pearl Harbor from four separate directions at the same time while the rest of the force circled.

Lieutenant Commander Kakuichi Takahashi, overall leader of the Aichi D3A1 Type 99 dive-bombers, led the attack against airfields prior to attacking the ships.[49]

At 0700, the assistant quartermaster on board the USS *Nevada* woke twenty-one-year-old Ensign Joseph K. Taussig Jr., the forenoon officer of the deck.[50] Ensign Taussig was the junior gunnery officer in charge of the starboard antiaircraft batteries.[51] His watch did not start until 0745, which gave him time to dress and eat breakfast.[52]

As Ensign Joseph K. Taussig, later to become secretary of the navy, looked around the deck, he noticed bluejackets lining up for the liberty party to shore. The ship's football team was tied for the championship, and they wanted a boat to Aiea Recreation Field. Ensign Taussig's messmates wanted a boat to Ford Island. In addition, the garbage lighter was standing in to take the garbage.[53] The crew were expecting a relaxing Sunday onshore.

Ensign Taussig called the log room and instructed them to light off another boiler.[54] The steaming boiler had been on for four days.[55]

0745

Ensign Joseph Taussig relieved the watch promptly at 0745.[56] His first duty of the day was to execute colors at 0800.[57]

0748

Japanese aircraft hit the seaplane base at Kaneohe Bay.[58] Duty officers made frantic calls to Bellow Field and Hickam Field. No one believed the bases were under attack. By the time the Japanese were finished strafing and bombing the navy's long-range reconnaissance planes, not one working plane was left.[59]

0749

Lieutenant Commander Kakuichi Takahashi's twenty-seven Aichi D3A1 Val dive-bombers from the carrier *Shokaku* attacked both Ford Island Naval Air Station and Hickam Army Airfield with 550-pound Type 98 general-purpose bombs.[60] Another twenty-seven dive-bombers from the carrier *Zuikaku* went after Wheeler Airfield and Schofield Barracks.[61] Forty-four Mitsubishi A6M Zero fighters provided an air canopy for the attacking bombers.[62]

A 550-pound bomb plowed through the roof of a 3,200-man barracks complex at Hickam, exploding in the dining room and killing thirty-five men eating breakfast.[63]

0751

Radio operator Dwayne L. Eskridge made the first report of Japanese aircraft.[64] He heard some low-flying planes and tapped out, "Standby," in Morse code.[65] Mr. Dwayne Eskridge described how he ran to the top of the two-story building he was working in. He said he could clearly see airplanes with red circles on each wing. Mr. Eskridge then ran downstairs and sent a message that Pearl Harbor was being bombed by Japanese planes.[66]

0750

Commander Fuchida and the Japanese aircraft approached Kahuku Point.[67] The main force then broke up into smaller groups, with each proceeding to its primary target. Commander Fuchida, in a Nakajima B5N torpedo bomber, remained with the high-level bombers. The USS *Nevada* was Commander Fuchida's prime target.[68]

CHAPTER 5

For me, my last day on earth began like most others. I awoke, got dressed, and went to the mess hall for chow. No one knows when death will come calling, and certainly none of us sailors had an inkling that many of us would die horrific deaths at the hands of Japanese treachery. Perhaps that was for the best. After all, do you want to know the exact moment and manner of your death? I think not, especially if you're going to burn to death in flaming oil while thrashing for life in the water, fry in the red-hot confines of a sealed steel compartment, or slowly suffocate in the cavernous depths of a capsized hull.

0755

It was the practice of our marine band to play "The Star-Spangled Banner" each Sunday morning on the fantail at colors while in port.[1] Bandleader Oden McMillian, his twenty-three musicians, and the marine color guard assembled on the aft deck, patiently waiting for the 0800 signal to begin.[2]

Ensign Joseph Taussig was too embarrassed to ask me what size flag to fly, so he quietly sent a man forward to see what they were going to do on the USS *Arizona*.[3] We ended up flying the same size flag as the *Arizona*.

After the USS *Pennsylvania* hoisted the blue peter, or prep flag, at 0755, I piped the preparatory signal for the hoisting of colors and the playing of the national anthem.[4] The crew began to see specks in the sky to the southwest. At first, we thought it was a training exercise.

Bandleader McMillan and his musicians saw planes bearing down on the other side of Ford Island. They heard muffled explosions and saw clouds of dirt and dust rise in the distance. That did not stop Mr. McMillan, who tapped his baton for his band to play "The Star- Spangled Banner" as the colors were hoisted.[5] Mr. McMillan and the marine band finished playing "The Star-Spangled Banner" with machine-gun fire directly overhead as a Japanese plane zoomed up over *Nevada*'s fantail. Even with machine-gun fire spraying the deck, not one musician broke formation until the final note sounded.[6] Then everyone, including me, immediately ran for cover.[7] Fortunately, the machine gunner missed the entire band as well as the marine color guard standing at attention in two rows.[8]

The first Japanese Kate torpedo bomber flew low over our deck, spraying it with twenty-millimeter cannon fire that shredded the American flag that had just been hoisted. The bravery and respect shown by Mr. McMillian, the marine band, and the color guard set the tone for the crew. Though the ensign was shredded, that did not stop the American colors from flying proudly. These colors do not run.

The navy yard signal tower telephoned Commander in Chief Pacific Fleet Headquarters: "Enemy air raid—not drill."[9] Almost simultaneously, Japanese torpedo planes attacked Battleship Row.[10]

Rear Admiral William Furlong was the commander of Battle Forces Pacific.[11] As Rear Admiral Furlong stood on the deck of the minelayer USS *Oglala,* a Japanese dive-bomber passed within six hundred feet of the ship.[12] At Rear Admiral Furlong's command, the USS *Oglala* flashed the alarm: "All ships in harbor sortie."[13] At 0758, Rear Admiral Patrick Bellinger radioed all ships: "Air raid on Pearl Harbor. This is not a drill."[14]

Our captain was not on board the *Nevada* during the attack. Captain Francis Worth Scanland had spent the night ashore in Waikiki—the first time he'd done so since *Nevada*'s arrival to Pearl Harbor in 1940.[15] His wife, married daughter, and baby granddaughter had arrived the previous day on the SS *Lureline.*[16] Captain Scanland had never met his granddaughter, and he had not seen his wife or daughter for more than a year.[17]

Executive Officer Harry L. Thompson was also ashore.[18] Command of the USS *Nevada* was then left to Lieutenant Commander Francis J. Thomas, a naval reservist who had joined the ship on June 22, 1941.[19] Mr. Thomas was the most senior officer present on the ship.[20]

One of our buglers began to anxiously announce general quarters on his own initiative before the order was issued.[21] Deafening explosions drowned out the bugler's call.[22] Ensign Joseph Taussig grabbed the bugler's horn and pulled the alarm bell.[23] Then he repeatedly shouted into the PA system, "All hands general quarters! Air raid! This is no drill!"[24] All seamen are familiar with the call "General quarters, general quarters. All hands man your battle stations!"

A gunner's mate third class, Leonard Wade, was tossed out of his bunk by the roar of exploding Japanese bombs.[25] Mr. Wade hurried to his battle station, which was the number-one gun.[26] He was dismayed as he quickly realized the ammunition had been removed the day before. Longer projectiles were to replace the current ammunition.[27] In the meantime, each of the guns had three sand-filled projectiles, which were useless against the attacking Japanese planes.[28]

Another crew member, Kenneth Herndon, ran to his battle station at one of the turret guns.[29] Just as Mr. Wade had discovered the useless sand projectiles in the guns, Mr. Herndon did not see any point in remaining where he was, so he went down to the magazine and brought up .50-caliber ammunition for the guns.[30]

Our crew had replaced their fourteen-inch shells as part of the normal ammunition rotation on Saturday, December 6.[31] It was planned for the crew to load the 2,800 bags of smokeless powder into the main magazines on Monday, December 8.[32]

It happened that on the morning of December 7, crew members were taking the temperatures of the ammunition ready boxes,[33] which meant that fortuitously, all ammunition boxes were unlocked, with the exception of the .50-caliber machine gun ammunition.[34] It was much quicker for crew members to knock the locks off the .50-caliber ammunition boxes than to wait for the keys.[35]

I grabbed a machete and cut the ropes holding up the awnings covering the guns along the deck.[36] This allowed the crew to return fire almost immediately.[37]

Even with all the difficulties with the guns and the ammunition, the USS *Nevada*'s crew distinguished themselves with their superb skills, despite overwhelming circumstances.

0802

We were ordered by Admiral Isaac Kidd on the USS *Arizona* to make all preparations to get underway.[38] Meanwhile, Chief Quartermaster Robert Sedberry relayed the order to the engine room.[39]

I looked out at the harbor, and it looks as if the entire harbor was in flames. The oil and water were like a spreading lake of fire. Blacks, reds, and yellows were all over, along with the sulfurous smell of burning fuel. There was deafening noise from all the bombs. The crew could barely hear each other.

Two Japanese Kate torpedo planes approached us.[40] Marines were able to shoot one of the planes down.[41] A sailor with a .30-caliber Lewis machine gun was credited with shooting down another.[42] A Japanese long-lance torpedo struck our portside hull between turrets one and two.[43] The explosion caused the ship to violently lurch upward with a vibrant shudder before slamming back onto the water.[44] We were all shaken, and I think I can safely say that every crew member was scared at that point, including me.

We refused to back down. Our crew fought courageously as we opened fire on enemy planes approaching the port beam.[45] One of the Kates was destroyed by our .50-caliber machine gun; it veered off, smoking, and then crashed about a hundred yards on the *Nevada*'s port quarter.[46] We all cheered. However, the plane managed to release its Type 91 torpedo before it crashed.[47]

Our cheers quickly turned to despair as we watched the torpedo silently streak toward our hull. *Boom!* A great shuddering of our ship occurred. The torpedo blast opened a large hole—sixteen feet by twenty feet by seven feet—in our port side, below our two forward turrets.[48] Our antitorpedo protection armor resisted the warhead's explosion fairly well.[49] However, the inmost bulkhead was leaking, allowing a considerable amount of water into the ship. Our ship was then pushed sideways away from the pier. After the hit we took, *Nevada* immediately listed to port.[50]

NH 64306 Pearl Harbor Attack. Hole in the ship's port side, between about frame 38 and frame 46, caused by a Japanese Type 91 aerial torpedo that hit her during the December 7, 1941, air raid. Photographed on about February 19, 1942, in Pearl Harbor Navy Yard's Drydock Number Two. The battleship's side armor is visible inside the hole's upper section. Official US Navy photograph from the collections of the Naval History and Heritage Command.

Photograph modified by Deborah Fritz—
cropped, clarified, and darkened.

0803

Fortunately, I had gone below deck for a few moments. From ten thousand feet above, a 1,760-pound armor-piercing bomb was dropped by a Japanese plane onto the USS *Arizona*.[51] The devastating bomb exploded next to the number-two turret, penetrating down to the ammunition magazine.[52] Seven seconds later, a shocking secondary explosion blew the battleship in half, killing 1,177 of the 1,512 men aboard, including Rear Admiral Isaac Kidd and Captain Franklin Van Valkenburg.[53] The bomb exploded in a fuel-storage compartment, and the fire spread to a magazine full of black powder.[54]

USS *Arizona* (BB-39) sunk and burning furiously on December 7, 1941. Her forward magazines exploded when she was hit by a Japanese bomb. At left, men on the stern of USS *Tennessee* (BB-43) are playing fire hoses on the water to force burning oil away from their ship. Official US Navy photograph in the collections of the National Archives. Photograph modified by Deborah Fritz—cropped for a better view of the *Arizona*.

The shock waves generated by the explosions reached our decks, causing intense heat from the blasts.[55] We were showered with searing metallic debris, which burned many of the crew.[56] If I had been topside, I most likely would have been badly burned too. The bomb that hit the USS *Arizona* was followed by a concussion that bent and warped our bridge wings and bulkheads with its intense heat.[57] I started feeling anxious but refused to show it in front of my men.

I was proud of our crew. Everyone was truly a hero in his own right. Poor Mr. Taylor's eardrums were perforated from the *Arizona*'s explosion, and he wasn't the only one that happened to. Mr. Taylor was also burned and wounded by shrapnel, but he kept hosing down the ammunition boxes, which were exhibiting red heat due to the proximity of the fires.[58] Fire had already exploded one ready ammunition box in our starboard five-inch AA battery.[59]

Lieutenant Lawrence Ruff had been aboard the hospital ship USS *Solace*, attending Mass.[60] He heard a roar and rushed to the starboard porthole. There he witnessed the *Arizona* erupt into a ball of flame.[61] Immediately, Lieutenant Ruff commandeered one of *Solace*'s launches, leaving Father Drinnan on the hospital ship.[62] I watched as the coxswain steered the launch to the USS *Nevada*. On the way, the launch rescued some of the men who had forcibly fallen off the *Nevada* and into the burning water when the USS *Arizona* exploded. As the small boat labored across the smoky harbor, the Japanese attempted to strafe it. Fortunately, the launch was not hit, as Lieutenant Ruff guided the coxswain under our stern for protection from the low-flying planes.[63] I assisted Lieutenant Ruff to quickly scramble up the ladder onto the quarterdeck.[64]

Pieces of the *Arizona* broke through *Nevada*'s portholes, even though she was moored more than two hundred feet away.[65] When I went to assist Lieutenant Ruff, I was told every man topside had been killed by the USS *Arizona*'s explosion.[66] I was devastated. Tears came to my eyes. They had been my coworkers and friends.

Ensign Joseph K. Taussig calmly issued orders while guiding his gun director from target to target.[67] Suddenly, a projectile smashed into Ensign Taussig's director and passed through his left thigh and right into the director's ballistic computer.[68] He had been standing in a doorway, holding tightly on to the doorknob to keep from falling. Ensign Taussig's left leg was shattered, with his foot embedded in his left armpit.[69] Ensign

Taussig stood on his right leg and started twisting the dials of his director set, which would not work.[70] Ensign Taussig soon fell out of the gun director, twisting in order to break his fall.[71] His men carefully picked him up and carried him to safety, away from the gun blasts and into the fire control shack. They gingerly laid Ensign Taussig on the deck. Fortunately, Ensign Taussig did not feel pain at that time and recalled how his left leg felt as if it had "gone to sleep."[72] A pharmacist's mate administered morphine to Ensign Taussig.[73] His wound was so high that a tourniquet would not hold. He had to hold his thigh closed with his hands to control the bleeding. *Poor kid,* I thought, but I knew he was tough, as he was the son of an admiral. Ensign Joseph Taussig was later awarded the Navy Cross for his heroism.

Ensign Taussig refused to be relieved of his duty as gun control officer.[74] Mr. Taussig attempted to regain control of the gun mounts. Most of the connections between Mr. Taussig's director and the starboard guns were lost, but he continued to give visual spotting reports over his sound-powered phones.[75] When I went to check on Ensign Taussig, I was shocked when I saw his leg, but I put on an expressionless face.

Thick, acrid black smoke spiraled upward from the *Arizona.*[76] It became difficult to breathe, and our throats were burning. Small rescue craft moved cautiously around burning oil while personnel pulled burned survivors out of the water. When I saw their burns, the sight made me feel sick inside.

As Ensign Joseph K. Taussig nervously smoked a cigarette, he felt a terrific jar.[77] He had just been moved to a relatively safe place on the deck by his men.[78] Mr. Taussig's cigarette had gone out, and he correctly surmised that a large bomb or a torpedo must have hit the ship. One of his men held up his head so he could see out the starboard door. Mr. Taussig felt frustrated and helpless because he was unable to supervise the firing.[79] Ensign Taussig's lookout reported that the tail had been shot from one of the planes.[80] The secondary battery had stopped firing. A bomb must have landed in the casemates.[81] The bomb had hit the number-four casemate.[82]

Ensign Joseph Taussig immediately ordered counterflooding.[83] Damage control then counterflooded four compartments on the starboard side.[84] Lieutenant Commander Frances Thomas did not want to chance the capsizing of an unbalanced ship.[85]

One of our crew members, Mr. George Hutton, explained how fortunate it was that the *Nevada* had been midway through a change in the type of ammunition used by the fourteen-inch guns.[86] Massive stockpiles of explosive powder had just been removed and not yet replaced.[87] Otherwise, when the torpedo struck the hull below the gun turrets, there would have been more fatalities.[88]

Our five-inch gun crews prevented a second torpedo from being launched when they scored a direct hit on another oncoming plane.[89] The plane disintegrated in midair, possibly because the five-inch shell detonated the torpedo's warhead.[90] The second torpedo slammed into the muddied bank.

A fire was raging on the *Nevada*'s bow, caused by the torpedo that had hit us. It was only getting worse, with the sheet of burning oil spreading from *Arizona*'s inferno.[91] My crew and I desperately tried to put the fire out.

Planes came swooping down, machine-gunning everything. Everyone hit the deck again as a crackling burst of bullets passed through the starboard overhead and on out the port bulkheads and open hatch.

The torpedo had knocked out the electric elevators on the port side of the ship. I knew we needed to immediately get more ammunition up to the guns. I organized a line of sailors, whoever was available. We passed ammunition up by hand from belowdecks to the guns.[92]

Ignited fuel oil on the surface of the water now threatened our ship, so "it was considered necessary to get underway to avoid further danger."[93]

Ensign Taussig said, "I had the second boiler fired up for two reasons. I wanted it up because I didn't like to be on a ship that couldn't get underway. I had been in the California earthquake in 1933, which made me conscious of a threat, so I tried, at all times, to be prepared. So whenever I took over the deck, I always fired up another engine."[94]

I knew there was nothing more vulnerable than a battleship tied to a quay during an attack of such proportions. If the *Nevada* was going to survive, we needed to get underway immediately.

0818

Time was running out. A sheet of flames from the *Arizona,* fueled by burning oil, spread across the water toward *Nevada*'s bow.[96]

The other battleships were unable to sortie, in part due to the lineup of ships in port and the fact that the battleships were tied together by twos.[97] Our ship was moored at the end of Ford Island by herself.[98] The USS *Arizona* had been moored alongside the USS *Vestal*. In being moored by ourselves, we had the advantage of being able to get away more easily than the other battleships.[99]

Not even a heavily armored battleship would be able to survive in a sea of burning oil for long.[100] It became clear to our seasoned officers that the USS *Nevada* needed to be moved, or we would risk losing the ship, and more importantly, many lives would be lost.[101]

Chief Warrant Officer Donald Ross and I began chopping lines and barking orders in order to get the USS *Nevada* moving.[102] Normally, this would have taken a leadership team of several officers, a harbor pilot, and four tugboats and two hours to accomplish.[103] Our team accomplished this in a matter of minutes.[104] The minimum steam to move a battleship required two boilers.[105] Boiler two was already in service to power auxiliary systems, and fires were lit under boilers one, three, four, and five.[106]

I knew exactly what was needed. Our ship had no chance to sortie without it being released from its mooring to the quay. I quickly asked some brave men if they would assist me to cut the lines from the ship to the quay. They knew the dangers of diving into hot oil with continual strafing. They volunteered anyway. We sprinted from the bridge and plunged forty feet from the stern into the hot, burning, oil-saturated water.[107] We winced as we hit the water. The smell was acrid. We saw bodies from the *Arizona* and the *Nevada* floating in the water. Huge geysers spouted from bombs being dropped. Spent antiaircraft shells fell into the water. It was a horrible job, but it couldn't be helped. My men and I had held on to several machetes when we jumped into the water. It was difficult to see with all the smoke. We slowly climbed up Quay Number 8; our clothes were heavy with the oil. The heavy rope mooring lines were thick. Lines from both the bow and the aft of the ship were attached to the cement quay, so there were several places to cut. Using our machetes, we hacked away with all our might, cutting through two feet of cordage. All around us, things were exploding, people were screaming, and Japanese Zeroes were strafing the water with machine-gun fire.

Lieutenant Lawrence Ruff found Chief Quartermaster Robert Sedberry on the bridge. On his own initiative, Mr. Sedberry had already ordered engineering to prepare to get underway.[108] Lieutenant Lawrence Ruff helped to lay out charts and identify navigable landmarks.[109]

Someone shouted, "Lay forward the anchor detail to get underway!" The lines were then being cast off forward, so they were starting to spring around on their stern lines. We heard the sickening swish and crash as the next bomb fell.

My men and I felt like sitting ducks. I felt responsible as some of my men died from the strafing. One man's body was lying in the hot oil. This was certainly not what I wanted. They were so brave. How was I going to tell their families?

Gebhard Galle raced down three decks to help get steam going to the engine room.[110] He opened a bypass valve for the steam to power the ship, which would help *Nevada* to get underway.[111]

Lieutenant Lawrence Ruff ordered the engines to "All ahead one-third," and Chief Quartermaster Robert Sedberry steered the ship to port and just cleared the USS *Vestal*, which was moored next to the burning *Arizona*.[112] At that point, our only communications with the rest of the ship were through the telegraph system, which was connected to the engine room, and the ship's JV voice-powered phones.[113]

0825

Lieutenant Lawrence Ruff then assumed the role of acting navigator, which he was not trained to do.[114] Lieutenant Commander Francis Thomas instructed Lieutenant Ruff to take charge of the ship and do his best to maneuver *Nevada* out of the harbor as quickly as possible, foregoing the usual protocol of a harbor pilot.[115]

With Lieutenant Commander Francis J. Thomas conning, Lieutenant Lawrence Ruff navigating, and Chief Quartermaster Robert Sedberry manning the helm, the USS *Nevada* was eased back from her berth.[116] Mr. Ruff aligned his landmarks on Ford Island and provided Mr. Thomas with positions and recommended courses to steer.[117]

0830

The sound of bending and cracking wood coming from my ship was noticeable as the thirty-two-thousand-ton ship began moving forward.[118] Lieutenant Commander Francis Thomas reached up and pulled the brass handle above his head, making one prolonged blast of *Nevada*'s whistle.[119] The ship then shuddered as her screws began churning up tons of water in an effort to stop her from going backward and send her forward.[120]

We had all six boilers off in ten minutes—record time. The *Nevada* was underway in eighteen minutes, steaming through the billowing smoke pouring from the *Arizona*.[121]

There was no way I was just going to sit there on the quay, drenched in hot oil, not doing anything. I needed to be with my ship. I told the other men I was going to swim back to the *Nevada*. I gave them the freedom to do whatever they wanted, as it was not fair to order them to participate any further in the dangerous mission. Three men came with me. We dove off the quay. Two of the men died in the water from severe burns. The other man and I swam with all our might to the *Nevada*. At first, no one saw or heard us amid all the smoke and noise. I felt helpless. Boatswain's Mate First Class Solar noticed us in the water and got us on board with ropes. I felt grateful to Mr. Solar and told him so.

As we passed the USS *Arizona*, the whole starboard side of the USS *Nevada* caught fire, causing injuries and fatalities. This was because the crew refused to leave their guns. All the antiaircraft officers except one were injured. All but three of the gun captains had been wounded or killed.[122] In addition, fourteen fires were burning.[123] Two of our crew members used their bodies as shields, protecting the ammunition from the intense heat of the *Arizona*. See what I mean? Our entire crew were heroes.

One *Arizona* radioman, Glenn Lane, had been in the water since the forward magazine explosion knocked him in at 0810, when his watch stopped.[124] He was trying to swim around the burning ship through oil-slicked water, when he saw the USS *Nevada*.[125] We rescued Mr. Lane, and he took up a battle station. Besides being covered in oil, fortunately, he had not been seriously injured except for a few burns.

I managed with some painful burns and bruises. I was covered in hot oil. I had to take my shoes off. I could not stand the hot oil on my uniform, as it was burning my skin further. I quickly went belowdecks to my quarters and changed into another uniform and a new pair of shoes.

The first wave of Japanese planes regrouped for the flight back to their aircraft carriers. This wave attack took less than forty minutes to execute.[126]

CHAPTER 6

Authorities ordered Lieutenant Commander Thomas to take the USS *Nevada* around the north end of Ford Island, for fear there might be mines south of *Nevada*'s berth.[1] However, by the time Mr. Thomas received the message, we were already committed to the direct route to the sea.[2]

We all felt an uneasy lull in the attacks at that point, which lasted for approximately twenty minutes.

All available hands were urgently called to help fight the multiple fires raging throughout our ship.

After we were beyond Battleship Row and down by the Ten-Ten Dock, named because of its 1,010-yard length, we encountered another obstacle.[3] Part of the channel was blocked by a long pipeline that ran out from Ford Island to the dredge *Turbine*. It was lying squarely in midstream.[4] Somehow, Chief Quartermaster Robert Sedberry maneuvered our ship between the dredge and the shore.[5] This maneuver was known as "threading the needle."[6] It was quite a feat for a ship without tugs.

I went back and forth topside, problem-solving, firefighting, and attempting to protect our crew as best as I could.

0850

After a ship gets underway, the American flag is transferred from the stern to the mast. There had been no time for us to move it. Our colors streamed proudly from the stern just the same.[7]

We began a southerly course along the eastern flank of Battleship Row. Crew members manning their battle stations could feel intense heat produced by the burning battleships.[8] The men on the ships cheered us on, and we were moved by the show of emotion.[9]

American servicemen across Pearl Harbor raised their heads in amazement as they saw us move around the burning USS *Arizona*; the sinking USS *West Virginia*; the capsized USS *Oklahoma*; the listing and burning USS *California*, Vice Admiral Pye's flagship; and the burning USS *Pennsylvania* in dry dock. Chief Quartermaster Robert Sedberry got our ship out in one of the greatest seamanship maneuvers of all time.[10]

I was proud of our crew and our ship. We were doing the impossible. What a great feeling. I think we inspired everyone in Pearl Harbor during that dark time, especially as we sailed with our guns blazing during the height of the first wave of the bombing.

NH 97396—Pearl Harbor Attack. USS *Nevada* (BB-36) headed down channel after being intensely attacked by Japanese dive-bombers. Photographed from Ford Island, with USS *Avocet* (AVP-4) in the foreground and the dredge line in the middle distance. Official US Navy photograph from the collections of the Naval History and Heritage Command. Photograph modified by Deborah Fritz—cropped, straightened, and clarified.

With heavy hearts, we watched what appeared to be a second wave of attack. We saw the planes returning.

When Commander Fuchida saw the USS *Nevada* defying the odds, emerging from the smoke and the haze, he was quoted as saying, "Ahh, good! ... Now just sink that ship right there!"[11] Five Japanese planes were diving toward the USS *Helena,* but when the aviators caught sight of our ship, they suddenly swerved in mid attack to converge on us.[12] We knew we were in for trouble. I had a funny feeling in my stomach.

Aichi Type 99 bombers from the Japanese carrier *Kaga* focused on us, hitting us with 250-kilogram bombs.[13] The Japanese rationalized that if they could sink us in the channel, it would seal Pearl Harbor up for months.[14]

Fortunately for us, at first, the Japanese aircraft dropped their bombs with little accuracy. Two bombs missed us, but a third one hit its mark.[15] It landed eleven inches from where Ensign John Landreth was inside the deck.[16] Explosions sounded, with two geysers of saltwater shooting up from the port side.

The other officers and I gave orders for ammunition boxes to remain completely filled and for guns to remain in the ready position. Although against navy regulations, the order allowed the gunners to return fire faster than any of the other ships.[17]

Japanese aircraft were swarming all over us. I did not have a good feeling.

0845

Our number-three and number-four boilers were relit as we cruised down the channel at almost nineteen knots. We exceeded the channel's posted limit of thirteen knots. However, in those circumstances, I don't think anyone cared.

0850

The fires on our bow were getting worse with the wind. Sailors stepped up to immediately replace fallen men. The remaining sailors continued to work the lines of communication, despite the power loss, flooding, and loss of oxygen in the lower decks.

Japanese dive-bombers opened up their attack on our forecastle deck, causing more leaks in our hull as well as starting gasoline fires forward and blazes in our superstructure and midship area.

0900

Things started to get really dicey when five big black bombs hit us in quick succession.[18] The noise was so loud! I tried to reassure some of the younger sailors. Three bombs hit the forecastle, penetrating the deck, and exploded below.[19] One of them exited the hull on the starboard side before detonating.[20] The explosion pressed the hull plate inward and started major flooding.[21] Another bomb passed through one of our gasoline tanks and out the bottom of the ship prior to exploding.[22] Fortunately, the bomb did not ignite the gasoline, but the breach in the gas tank released vapors that caused problems later.[23] The third bomb penetrated down to the second deck, bounced back up, and then blew a large hole in the deck.[24] Two bombs hit *Nevada*'s superstructure. One penetrated the port director platform in the foremast and then exploded on the upper deck, at the base of the stack.[25] The other exploded just above the crew's galley.[26]

The bomb that hit our superstructure penetrated four decks downward, tore a hole through Captain Scanland's cabin and detonated below.[27] The ready ammunition stored nearby exploded, sending a towering inferno that engulfed the entire area.

My friend Chief Warrant Officer Donald Ross was sitting below one of the air ducts in the forward dynamo room, when the blast hit him in the face.[28] The searing heat blinded him. Poisonous, acrid smoke poured into the compartment.[29] Chief Warrant Officer Ross ordered everyone out to prevent them from inhaling the dangerous fumes.[30]

One of our AA gun positions was now completely destroyed.[31] As I walked topside, I noticed fires were erupting throughout the boat deck and the ship's galley.[32] The firefighting unit lost water pressure when the pump to *Nevada*'s hoses was destroyed.[33] Flooding above the grilled floor plates of the number-one and number-two fire rooms was noted, and the rooms were secured.[34] Tugboats came off our starboard side and began shooting streams of water onto the raging fires.[35] Some of the extinguished fires flared up again as the hot metal reignited smoldering debris. It was a constant battle.

Lieutenant Commander Thomas spoke through the phones and then to his recorder, who worked over a clipboard full of scrap paper.[36] The recorder held up a cutaway configuration of *Nevada*'s hull shape, which showed all voids and compartments, to Lieutenant Commander Thomas.[37] Mr. Thomas erased or colored in various sections on the cutaway to indicate if fire and flooding were or were not under control. The large fire on the bow continued to rage. Lieutenant Commander Thomas ordered compartment Fox 14 blocked off, and compartment 15 flooded.[38] He was thinking about how to keep ballast as well as watertight integrity.[39] Mr. Thomas ordered the forward magazines to be hosed down. He issued a reminder for the crew to check and secure their life jackets.

Unless someone manned the forward dynamo room, the ship would lose electricity and the ability to fight back.[40] Electrical power could be shifted to the aft dynamo control room. Chief Warrant Officer Donald Ross struggled to maintain consciousness as he transferred the power to the aft dynamo control room. When the transfer was complete, Mr. Ross lost consciousness. I was alarmed when he was presumed dead. Fortunately, corpsmen revived him. I checked on him when he was brought topside to breathe fresh air. I was relieved he was going to be okay. I patted him on the shoulder. Chief Warrant Officer Ross would be awarded the Congressional Medal of Honor for his actions.

Ensign Thomas Taylor continued to run the port antiaircraft battery as best as he was able. Mr. Taylor was burned and was now deaf due to a blast rupturing his eardrums.[41]

I went to check on my friend Ensign Joseph Taussig. He told me his back was getting warm as he lay on a stretcher. Ensign Taussig asked me if there was a fire below deck on the navigation bridge. I confirmed this.

The telephone rang, and Ensign Taussig answered it. Our ship was ordered to run aground.[42] My friend and I both were upset by the intelligence. Directly after that, Ensign Taussig witnessed the paint on the sky-control bulkheads start to blister.[43] He ordered the men to abandon sky control, but he got no response.[44]

I felt the USS *Nevada* was lower in the water than she should have been. Our officers received a message by light, sent from the tower: "Do not block the harbor entrance! Do not block the harbor entrance!"[45] We were all concerned the USS *Nevada* would sink and block the channel, just as the Japanese wanted.

Lieutenant Lawrence Ruff, Lieutenant Commander Francis Thomas, Chief Quartermaster Robert Sedberry, and I formed a consensus, deciding to take our ship as near as possible to Hospital Point and beach her on the eastern side of the channel.[46]

Chief Quartermaster Robert Sedberry turned the wheel to port. We all sadly watched *Nevada*'s burning nose bear down on the YPO peninsula at that time. That was the green finger of land marking the West Lock. Hospital Point and a portion of the harbor entrance were coming into view through the port windows. The entrance was only one and a half miles from the open sea.[47] That was how close we had come to making it out of the harbor. We felt devastated, but we all understood the necessity of grounding the *Nevada*.

0907

Captain Scanland had left his home in Honolulu as the first bombs fell, fighting his way through the chaos. It seemed like forever to Captain Scanland as he slowly navigated his vehicle. Once he reached the dock, the captain boarded a yard tug, hoping it could take him to *Nevada*, which was making her way down the channel. Captain Scanland managed to rejoin us after we ran aground on Hospital Point, reassuming command.[48] He arrived just five minutes after Vice Admiral Pye had ordered the *Nevada* beached.[49]

On Hospital Point, the tide spun our ship completely around so that she faced Waipi'o Peninsula.[50] Admiral Furlong ordered two tugs to help us.[51] With the assistance of the tugs, we backed the *Nevada* up as far as we could in order to get a running start. Then she surged forward and plowed into the beaches of Hospital Point by a cane field. The tug *Hoga* and the tender *Avocet* poured streams of water onto the raging forecastle fire with four hose lines.[52]

As the USS *Nevada*'s bow began to grind on the bottom of Hospital Point, I was on the fantail, commanding my line handlers.[53] I ordered them to take cover when the *Nevada*'s stern was raked by strafing fire, which saved their lives.[54] I stayed out in the open, remaining at the anchor windlass with Boatswain's Mate First Class Solar.[55] We were attempting to let go of the stern anchor and secure the ship as she grounded.[56] A 550-pound bomb dropped from a Japanese D3A, pierced the deck, and exploded beneath our feet.[57]

The Japs were all over us. I didn't want to lose any more of my men, but that hope was dashed. Being responsible for those men—mostly teenagers the same age as my daughter—was a difficult moral obligation.

I thought, *Even though I am a husband and a father, God comes first. I will come through this if he wants me to. If not, I trust he will carry my family. Oh, my family. I don't want anything to happen to them. I love them so much.*

To the job on hand. I must get to the anchor. I must. I will do it, as I do not want to risk other lives. Enough have been killed. Enough!

Strafing was all over the place. I could hear the bullets whiz by my head. *Weird.*

I reached the anchor. I had to get it out to keep the *Nevada* stable. *She must not block the channel. Who knows what else the Japs have in mind. They are decimating us.* I suddenly felt sharp, heavy pains in my right shoulder, my left leg, and then my back. Searing, hot, heavy, sharp—kind of like walking into a hornets' nest. Then there was an explosion beneath me.

So strange. I felt a pushing out of my body. Suddenly, I felt so light. *Weird.* What was going on? I could see my poor broken body in the water.

The concussion was so strong that my body was blown overboard. *I can see all that is happening. I don't feel pain. I didn't feel a thing when the bomb hit. Oh God, the men. Look at all the bodies. Some were blown overboard, as I was. Now I see the body parts. This is too awful to visualize. Am I dead? Wow, so strange. I think I am. But yet I am right here!*

* * *

I am Chief Warrant Officer Ross, and I will continue the story from here. I was still topside, getting fresh air. Chief Boatswain Hill was attending to the anchor with Mr. Solar helping him. I witnessed the explosion that killed them both. As I sat resting, I immediately thought of Catherine and their three children. How were they going to manage? I didn't do it often, but I started to cry. I took a glance at Ensign Taussig, who was also crying.

We lost a great man that day. Edwin Hill was the senior warrant officer and chief boatswain's mate on the USS *Nevada* when I came aboard on November 18, 1940.[58] He was also the advancement officer and in charge of training all through the deck divisions. And he knew more about damage control than any first lieutenant.[59]

Eddie Hill was also a wonderful leader, not only for the men but also for the other officers, who respected him. He was the most outstanding man on the ship—in fact, on any ship I've ever been on.[60]

Ensign Joseph Tausig shared his remembrance of Chief Boatswain Hill during an interview, saying, "I don't know much about his personal background, except that I do know that no man makes chief warrant officer without being totally outstanding."[61] Seamen serving on the USS *Nevada* regarded Chief Boatswain Hill with the highest level of respect, equal to the captain himself.[62] The crewmen unquestioningly followed Chief Boatswain Hill, as he exuded authority and had thirty years of naval experience.[63]

Ensign Joseph Knefler Taussig Jr., later a captain, described, in an interview with William Kelly, Chief Boatswain Hill's concern in training young officers on the USS *Nevada*.[64] Ensign Taussig said the entire crew admired him, and Chief Boatswain Hill won almost every sailing award in the navy. Chief Warrant Officer Donald Ross and Mr. Taussig both remembered Chief Boatswain Hill as a great teacher and said he loved to instruct others on how to sail.[65]

Mr. Herndon said in a later interview, "He [Mr. Hill] was my boss. He was chief warrant boatswain, and all the people on deck force came under his direction. He was very strict, just, and very knowledgeable. He had over twenty years in the navy at the time of the attack. Hill was a leader; it's just that simple. He was respected by everybody up and down the ranks. The admirals had just as much respect for him as I had. That's the kind of gentleman he was. He ran a tight ship."[66]

Mr. William West said, "He [Mr. Hill] came up through the ranks and was the chief boatswain, which, is probably as important a position as the captain ... He was somebody you could look up to. A fine and upright professional navy man. He was good looking, straight as a ramrod, and commanded respect from everyone who knew him. He was a brave man, what every navy man should be. Everything about him was navy, and everyone respected him, from seamen to admirals. And you called him Mr. Hill, by God."[67]

Chief Warrant Officer Jim Wright (who did not serve on the USS *Nevada*) said that when he was a chief petty officer and later a chief warrant officer, he used to tell Chief Boatswain Edwin Hill's story to the chief petty officer candidates during their initiation.[68] Mr. Wright described how a chief's initiation changes a sailor into someone he never thought possible.[69] Wright said, "In order to be a chief warrant officer, a sailor must have to be a chief first."[70]

NH 49196. Chief Boatswain Edwin Joseph Hill, USN, who was awarded the Medal of Honor posthumously for heroism while serving on board USS *Nevada* (BB-36) during the December 7, 1941, Japanese raid on Pearl Harbor. Halftone-reproduction, copied a publication. US Naval History and Heritage Command photograph.

Chief Boatswain Hill's body was recovered on the port side of the ship at Hospital Point by a second-class pharmacist mate. The pharmacist mate told me, "When I picked up his body, there wasn't a bone that wasn't broken."[71]

The tide and the wind were pushing our ship up and lifting her up off the mud at Hospital Point.[72] *Nevada*'s stern started to swing toward the harbor entrance, acting like a closing gate.[73] Orders were quickly given for harbor tugs to assist us up out of the mud at Hospital Point and beach her against the side of the Waipi'o Peninsula.[74] The peninsula was opposite the Ford Island seaplane ramp, on the western side of the channel.[75] The tugs pushed our stern around until her bow slid free.[76] They then accompanied us across the channel to Waipi'o Peninsula, which was located about a half mile from Hospital Point.[77] At Waipi'o Point, the USS *Nevada* was grounded by her stern, with her bow directed down channel, alongside channel buoy number nineteen.[78] She was then beached and settled in shallow water.[79] With only her stern on the coral shelf, our ship continued to take on water through her bow and middle section.[80]

USS *Nevada* (BB-36) aground and burning of Waipi'o Point after the end of the Japanese air raid. Ships assisting her, at right, are the harbor tug *Hoga* (YT-146) and USS *Avocet* (AVP-4). Official US Navy photograph in the collections of the National Archives. Catalog 80-G-33020.

Captain Scanland sent Lieutenant Lawrence Ruff to Commander in Chief Pacific Fleet Headquarters in order to report the initial damage assessment.[81] Lieutenant Ruff related that at least one torpedo and five bombs had hit the *Nevada*, mostly on her forward sections.[82] Numerous near misses had added to her hull damage.[83] The engineering department was flooded. Stubborn fires were still burning at that time and would not be extinguished until 1800.[84] The grand USS *Nevada* was now neither battle-worthy nor seaworthy.[85]

* * *

Seaman Second Class Charles Sehe speaking. I recall how the USS *Nevada* still lay bow down, mired in the mud.[86] Along with crew members, I began throwing loose debris and metal fragments onto the barges. In the meantime, repair crews from the navy yard climbed aboard, carrying acetylene torch tanks.[87] They cut through the fire-blackened, torn, and twisted structures.[88]

* * *

Chief Warrant Officer Donald Ross speaking. Commander Fuchida unsuccessfully argued for a third wave of attack.[89] The Japanese bombers focused on a moving target, the USS *Nevada*.[90] As a result of their being distracted by the *Nevada*, the fuel oil tanks, dry docks, and shipyard were not hit.[91] If those targets had been destroyed, it would have been necessary for the Pacific Fleet to retreat to California.[92] It would have taken the United States at least two years to restore the 6.5 million barrels of lost fuel oil if the fuel tanks had been destroyed.[93]

According to the Annual Sanitary Report for 1941 from the USS *Nevada*, 116 men were injured severely enough to require hospitalization, 33 were known to be dead, and 18 were missing.[94]

CHAPTER 7

It was a cloudy and damp morning on December 8, 1941. Catherine Hill had been up all night. When Eddie had told Catherine to take the children to Cape May because of rising tensions between Japan and the United States, they'd left Long Beach. Two weeks prior, a relative had driven them to the East Coast. He had taken them directly to the Windsor Hotel.

There was a large radio in the lobby of the hotel. Everyone staying in the Windsor gathered around the radio, listening all afternoon and evening, when word arrived the Japanese were attacking Pearl Harbor. Rumors abounded, some true and many false. Catherine was worried. In fact, she was suffering from acute anxiety. Fear and excitement filled the entire country. The children—young Catherine, then nineteen; Eddie Jr., fifteen; and Michael, seven—sensed the tension and worry. Edwin Jr. was awakened at seven thirty in the morning by his mother. She instructed him to run to the store two blocks away to be there when it opened at eight o'clock and buy a newspaper. The radio was already back on.

Eddie returned and brought the newspaper to his mother. She read the front page. Between the paper and the radio, information was scattered. Catherine learned the Japanese had attacked Pearl Harbor; the battleship *West Virginia* had sunk; the USS *Oklahoma* had overturned; and a third battleship, not named, had sunk. The paper reported about one hundred killed. More articles spoke of Britain declaring war on Japan, and the Japanese had launched a second attack on the Philippines.

The day dragged on as, once again, everyone in the Windsor Hotel listened to the big radio. Catherine had to take a walk outside to get some fresh air. The waiting and the tension were getting to be too much. Was Eddie okay? Was he dead? Was he in a hospital somewhere, asking for her? What should she tell the children? She really couldn't tell them much, because she didn't know anything. Catherine hated that her children too were stressed and worried about their dad's safety. Thank goodness they were far away from Hawaii. Eddie had been right. He'd had an underlying feeling something was going to happen with Japan.

The lobby door opened, and in walked a naval messenger delivering a telegram. Whom was it for? Was it bad or possibly good news? Would it tell them more about what was going on? Would it tell them if the United States was at war? The messenger went to the front desk and asked Rose Hill if there was a Mrs. Edwin J. Hill present. Her immediate thought was *Oh no, something bad happened to Eddie.* Young Catherine, Eddie Jr., and Michael rose from the chairs in which they were sitting. Catherine noted they looked exhausted, just how she felt. All three had circles under their eyes. Would this be the feared telegram all military wives dreaded?

Catherine walked toward the naval messenger and said, "I'm Mrs. Edwin J. Hill." He handed the telegram to her with sympathy in his eyes, but he did not wait for her to open it, as there were many other similar telegrams to deliver. Catherine closed her eyes as she opened the telegram.

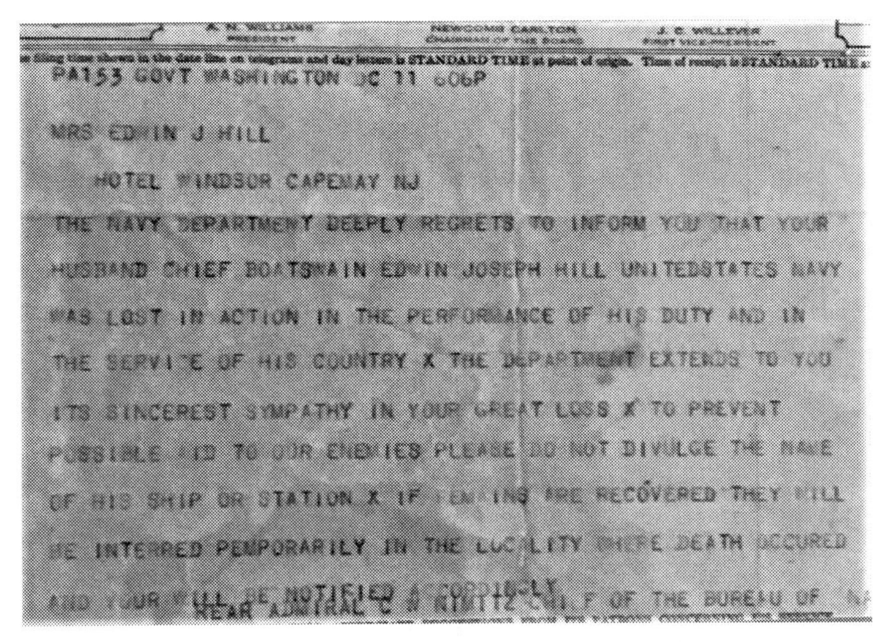

PA153 GOVT WASHINGTON DC 11 606P

MRS EDWIN J HILL

HOTEL WINDSOR CAPEMAY NJ

THE NAVY DEPARTMENT DEEPLY REGRETS TO INFORM YOU THAT YOUR HUSBAND CHIEF BOATSWAIN EDWIN JOSEPH HILL UNITEDSTATES NAVY WAS LOST IN ACTION IN THE PERFORMANCE OF HIS DUTY AND IN THE SERVICE OF HIS COUNTRY X THE DEPARTMENT EXTENDS TO YOU ITS SINCEREST SYMPATHY IN YOUR GREAT LOSS X TO PREVENT POSSIBLE AID TO OUR ENEMIES PLEASE DO NOT DIVULGE THE NAME OF HIS SHIP OR STATION X IF REMAINS ARE RECOVERED THEY WILL BE INTERRED TEMPORARILY IN THE LOCALITY WHERE DEATH OCCURED AND YOUR WILL BE NOTIFIED ACCORDINGLY

REAR ADMIRAL C W NIMITZ CHIEF OF THE BUREAU OF NA

Courtesy of William Furey, from his personal collection.

"Oh my Lord and the Blessed Mary, save me." With that, Catherine collapsed onto the floor.

Rose and the children ran immediately to her side. Rose snapped at her brother William, "Get a glass of water and tissues—now!" Then Rose spoke in a firm voice to the help. "Prepare a clean bed at once in the closest room available, because Catherine's room is on the second floor. That is too far. Now!"

As Catherine awoke to the nightmare, Rose and William helped her to her feet. The children were crying and trying their best to hold it together. Rose handed Catherine the glass of water. All she could manage was a sip. Catherine kept repeating, "Oh God. Oh God. Oh God." Rose and William guided Catherine to the freshly prepared room. Catherine immediately fell onto the bed. She just wanted to sleep to escape from the nightmare. She desperately clutched a Cape May diamond necklace Eddie had given her. What was she going to do without Eddie?

As Rose and William left the room, Rose said, "We will close the door and check on you very soon. Rest, my sweet, dear Catherine. We will care for the children. Do not worry yourself about them."

Catherine could not even comfort her own children because of the great depth of pain in her spirit. As she was thinking that, Catherine drifted off into a fitful sleep.

* * *

Chief Boatswain Hill speaking. I expressed to God my concerns for my family. My beautiful wife, Catherine—oh, how I love her. Our children, whom God graciously gave us. What will happen to them? I am not with them now. I don't ever want to leave this place, heaven, because it is my true home. I know this. I have always known this. Yet I need my family.

God reassures me in a way only He can. Suddenly, I feel my free spirit flying through the heavens and the earth. I see Catherine crying. I hug her. I know she can't see me. Can she feel me? Can she sense my presence? I hug her as tightly as a bodiless spirit can hug a person. Wait. She smiles. She hugs me back and says, "I love you, Edwin Joseph Hill. I will always love you. Thank you for the time we had together. My heart aches for you, yet I know you are with Jesus. Thank you."

Next, I am taken to my daughter, Catherine. She is also crying. I gently attempt to wipe her tears, but they still flow. I tell her I love her and will be waiting for her in heaven.

I feel myself going to my son Eddie. I hug him and express to him how much I love him and how proud of him I am. I tell him I will always be with him.

Next, I go to Michael, my youngest. He is seven years old, and he is trying hard to hold it together, especially for his mother. I whisper into his ear that I love him. I ask him to always remember me and to tell his descendants about me.

From left to right: Michael, Catherine, and Edwin Hill Jr. Photograph courtesy of Patricia Tiegen.

I ask the readers to please not forget the Pearl Harbor attack. Do not ever forget those on the USS *Arizona*. Do not ever forget how we fought for America's freedom, upheld justice, and tried our best to protect our country from evil forces. Please do not forget my favorite ship, the *Nevada*. She was a strong ship who protected us the best she could. I see how she distinguished herself throughout the war. The USS *Nevada* will somehow always be part of me. I am honored to have been written about and spoken about and to have had a ship and a camp named after me. I am proud of the memorials set up for me, especially the one in Cape May. When you pass by, please do not just walk by. Stop. Please take the time to read what it says.

My dearest Catherine has come to me, along with our daughter and our son Edwin. I see the beautiful spirits of our twin boys and our Mary

Helen. Though their deaths nearly broke Catherine and me, they are grown and full of joy and love here. Even the dog we had as children in Cape May is here. May our Lord and Savior bless and keep you all.

Please, America, keep us in your hearts. Remember me and my men. It has been said that history repeats itself. I witnessed the dying souls on September 11, 2001, from heaven. All heaven wept. The author's father, William George Fischer, told his daughter on 9/11 that it was worse than Pearl Harbor. I only know that the two days can be compared, with the loss of many innocent lives.

It is your job to teach our future generation about these days. Though Pearl Harbor survivors are few and will soon all be gone, please never forget us.

Pray for our world leaders. Pray for the current president of the United States. Pray for our nation. Always have hope. Keep on your life's journey, though it may be arduous and filled with much pain. Please do not allow evil forces to take over America. Even more importantly, do not ever let the evil come from within our country. The United States will stand united. I send love to you all.

EPILOGUE

Even though Chief Boatswain Hill did not survive the battle, his mission was ultimately a success. Chief Boatswain Hill's actions during the attack were inspirational not only to the personnel stationed in Pearl Harbor but to all. Through Chief Boatswain Hill's bravery, the USS *Nevada* survived to be one of three battleships able to continue fighting. The *Nevada* participated in seven major military engagements in World War II, making a significant impact in turning the tide of the war for the Allies.[1]

The official citation for the Congressional Medal of Honor Chief Boatswain Edwin J. Hill received for his heroism that day indicated he had been killed by the bomb that struck the bow.[2] However, according to the Pearl Harbor Visitors Bureau, bullet wounds found on his body suggest he could have been killed by strafing fire.[3]

Catherine was given the choice of having her husband's grave moved to Washington, DC, or keeping his grave in Hawaii. Though Mrs. Hill had never seen Hawaii, she had heard of the beauty of the Punchbowl

Cemetery. She made the decision for her husband to rest in that beautiful and peaceful place.[4] Plus, he would be surrounded by his shipmates. Catherine felt her husband would have been happiest in that promised land, so to speak.[5]

WWII

Edwin Joseph Hill

Chief Boatswain
U.S. Navy

Interred:
Section A, Grave #895

ORGANIZATION: U.S. Navy
U.S.S. Nevada

PLACE AND DATE:
Pearl Harbor, Hawaii, 7 December 1941

ACCREDITED TO: Pennsylvania

DATE AND PLACE OF BIRTH:
4 October 1895, Philadelphia, Pennsylvania

DATE OF DEATH: 7 December 1941

Citation: For distinguished conduct in the line of his profession, extraordinary courage, and disregard of his own safety during the attack on the Fleet in Pearl Harbor, by Japanese forces on 7 December 1941. During the height of the strafing and bombing, Chief Boatswain Hill led his men of the line-handling details of the U.S.S. Nevada to the quays, cast off the lines and swam back to his ship. Later, while on the forecastle, attempting to let go the anchors, he was blown overboard and killed by the explosion of several bombs.

Courtesy of William Furey, from his personal collection.

Statue of Lady Columbia at the National Cemetery of the Pacific, located within the Puowaina Crater. Photograph by Deborah Fritz, 1990.

Photograph courtesy of Peter Hill, from his personal collection.

Chief Boatswain Hill is buried in the National Memorial Cemetery of the Pacific, Honolulu, Hawaii, in section A, grave 895.[6]

Chief Warrant Officer Edwin J. Hill's Congressional Medal of Honor Citation

For distinguished conduct in the line of his profession, extraordinary courage, and disregard of his own safety during the attack on the Fleet in Pearl Harbor by Japanese forces on Dec. 7, 1941. During the height of the strafing and bombing, Chief Boatswain Hill led his men of the line handling details of the USS *Nevada* to the quays, cast off the lines and swam back to his ship. Later, while on the forecastle, attempting to let go the anchors, he was blown overboard and killed by the explosion of several bombs.[7]

Painting by Steve Mogck, Mr. and Mrs. William Furey's son-in-law, from their personal collection. The writing in the background is from the letters Chief Warrant Officer Hill wrote to his family. (Note: Chief Boatswain Hill is shown wearing his Congressional Medal of Honor, but in reality, he never got to see the medal awarded to him.)

ape May has close tie to Pearl Harb

ngressional Medal of Honor winner Chief Botswain Edwin J. Hill, U.S. Navy,

ny summers in Cape May. His family was here when they received the horribl

Reprinted with written permission by the *Cape May Star and Wave*. From William Furey's collection.

STAR & WAVE 8/13/70

To Name Walks After War Dead

The city intends to honor its war dead by naming three downtown walkways after distinguished servicemen who gave their lives for their country, and city fathers on Monday selected the first name.

Edwin J. Hill will be the first name bestowed upon one of the walkways connecting the service streets with the proposed Washington Street Mall.

Chief Boatswain Hill was awarded the Medal of Honor posthumously for distinguished action aboard the USS Nevada during the attack on Pearl Harbor in 1941.

Born in Philadelphia, Hill later established his legal address at the Hotel Windsor which at the time was operated by his aunt, Rose Halpin.

In addition to receiving the Congressional Medal of Honor, Hill also had the posthumous honor of having the Naval training center at Farragut, Idaho and a destroyer launched in 1943 named in his honor. This combination of three major honors may not have been paralleled by those of any other American in World War II.

Hill was married here at Our Lady Star of the Sea Church to Catherine Coughlin of Queenstown, Ireland. Years later one of his four children was fatally burned at the Windsor Hotel.

Hill's name was selected by the Mayor's Advisory Committee and was supported by the Cape May Citizens' Association.

The Mayor's Advisory Committee has contacted the local American Legion and VFW posts for names of deceased members so that names for the two other walkways can be selected for a possible dedication ceremony on Veteran's Day in November.

STAR & WAVE 9/3/70

ormer Newsboy nstrumental In Naming Walkway

A former Star and Wave ewsboy who remembered selling a particular issue of the ewspaper years ago was instrumental in having the first Irban Renewal walkway amed in honor of Edwin J. Hill.

Chief Boatswain Hill, a local resident, was awarded the Medal of Honor posthumously for distinguished action aboard the USS Nevada during the attack on Pearl Harbor.

At the time of Hill's death, Edward J. Haggerty, now an area real estate salesman, was a newsboy for the Star and Wave and sold an issue of the paper carrying Hill's obituary to Hill's sister, Mrs. Charles (Rose) Furey.

Last winter Haggerty recalled this incident of 1941 when he read in the Star and Wave that the city was to select two names for the service streets.

Haggerty contacted Walter Measday, chairman of the Mayor's Advisory Committee, and suggested Hill's name. By that time, however, the committee had already selected the name Lyle Lane.

The name of Hill was later selected as the committee's first choice for the first of three names for the walkways between the service streets and the proposed Washington street mall.

Reprinted with written permission from the *Cape May Star and Wave*. From David B. Hill Jr.'s personal collection.

Mall Walk To Honor Edwin Hill

CAPE MAY — A walkway in the urban renewal mall area will be named after Chief Boatswain's Mate Edwin J. Hill, who died at Pearl Harbor, Mayor Frank A. Gauvry announced at Monday morning's City Council meeting.

The decision was made by the Mayor's Advisory Committee for Civic Improvement, he added, with the citizens' association concurring.

"It has been decided to honor a deceased member of the U.S. Navy, who posthumously received the Congressional Medal of Honor," Gauvry said.

Hill, was on the "Nevada" at Pearl Harbor at the time of the Japanese attack, and received the medal for his distinguished action **there.**

The USS Destroyer "Hill" was also named after the Cape May native, the mayor pointed out.

Reprinted with written permission from the *Cape May Star and Wave*. Courtesy of David B. Hill Jr.'s personal collection.

CAPE MAY'S

WASHINGTON ST. MALL

WALKWAY DEDICATION

HONORING EDGAR ARTHUR DRAPER, M. D.
COLONEL HENRY WASHINGTON SAWYER
CHIEF BOATSWAIN EDWIN J. HILL, CMH

AUGUST 12, 1971
11:00 A. M.

Cape May dedicates the Washington Street Walkways today not just to notable men in its past, but to people everywhere who exhibit the Benchmarks of Great Men: Honor, Courage and Humility. These are the traits that are worthy of dedication.

D. R. Heacock

Courtesy of David B. Hill Jr.'s personal collection.

AT HILL WALK

(Adjacent to 418 Washington St.)
Honoring Chief Boatswain Edwin J. Hill, CMH
1895 - 1941

NARRATIVE
UNVEILING OF PLAQUES .... Deputy Mayor, Bernard A. Berk
SELECTION—
"Eight Bells and All Is Well" .... Hill-Noble
Lyrics written by Mr. Hill in 1941 shortly before Japanese Attack on Pearl Harbor

Special Note: The Glassboro College Music Corps will present a program of Music including Jr. Band, Senior Band and Chorus at 7:30 tonight at the Hill Walkway. Everyone is invited.

Courtesy of David B. Hill Jr.'s personal collection.

Chief Boatswain Hill wrote the lyrics to a song entitled "Eight Bells and All Is Well." George Noble composed the music to Mr. Hill's lyrics.[8] Chief Boatswain Edwin Hill was honored with his song being played during the dedication of the walk and memorial.[9]

Photograph taken by Deborah Fritz, May 2019.

There is a small monument dedicated to Chief Warrant Officer Edwin J. Hill, just off the Washington Street Mall in Cape May. On December 7, 1991, local veterans held a small ceremony at the monument dedicated to him.[10]

Cape May Memorial honoring Chief Boatswain Edwin Joseph Hill, located on Hill Walk in Washington Street Mall. Note that the memorial's title appears to say, "World War I Hero." Unfortunately, the second *I* for *World War II* fell off. It should read, "World War II Hero." Photograph by Deborah Fritz, May 2019.

In 1943, the United States Navy named a destroyer escort the USS *Hill* (DE-141) in Mr. Hill's memory.[14] Catherine Hill launched the USS *Hill* at the Consolidated Steel Corporation plant in Orange, Texas, on February 8, 1943.[15] That ship has since been decommissioned.[16]

From
ELEVENTH NAVAL DISTRICT
Public Relations Office
Los Angeles

Serial No. LA (a)-156(43)

FOR IMMEDIATE RELEASE

The destroyer escort vessel USS HILL, named in honor of Edwin Joseph Hill, chief Boatswain, U.S. Navy, will be launched at the Consolidated Steel Corp. Ltd, Orange, Texas, shipyard on February 28.

Sponsor of the new ship will be Mrs. Catherine J. Hill, 4209 Theresa Avenue, Long Beach, the widow of Chief Boatswain Hill who lost his life at Pearl Harbor on December 7, 1941.

Chief Boatswain Hill was awarded the Medal of Honor posthumously by the President of the United States in the name of Congress with the following citation:

"For distinguished conduct in the line of his profession, extraordinary courage and disregard of his own safety during the attack on the Fleet in Pearl Harbor, T.H., by Japanese forces on December 7, 1941. During the heighth of the strafing and bombing he led his men of the line handling details of a warship to the quays, cast off lines, and swam back to his ship. Later, while on the forecastle attempting to let go the anchors, he was blown overboard and killed by the explosion of several bombs."

Chief Boatswain Hill had the Mexican service medal and the Victory medal with mobile clasp for service in the USS MELVILLE during the first World War.

--------aec--------

Courtesy of David B. Hill Jr., from his personal collection. Notice the end of the document states Chief Boatswain Edwin J. Hill also received the Mexican Service Medal and the Victory Medal with clasp for service on the USS *Melville* during World War I.

Consolidated Steel Corporation, Ltd.
Cordially invites you to be present
at the launching of the
U. S. S. Hill
for the
United States Navy
Sunday, February 28, 1943
11:00 A.M.
Orange, Texas

Sponsor
Mrs. Catherine J. Hill

R.s.v.p.

Courtesy of Commander Edwin Furey,
from his personal collection.

Besides a destroyer tender named after Chief Boatswain Hill, a camp in the Farragut Naval Training Station was named after him.[11] The camp was thirty miles north of Coeur d'Alene, Idaho.[12] This training station was the second-largest naval training base in the world during World

War II.[13] Seven camps made up the naval training center: Bennion, Ward, Waldron, Hill, Scott, Peterson, and Gillmore.[14] Each of the camps was named after a navy hero killed in action.[15] The camps were inspected by President Roosevelt in the fall of 1942.[16] However, the base was decommissioned in 1946.[17]

The USS *Nevada* Report of Pearl Harbor Attack, written on December 15, 1941, by Captain Scanland to the Commander-in-Chief Pacific Fleet Headquarters, said,

> Chief Boatswain E. J. Hill, US Navy, killed in action, is deserving of the highest commendation possible to be given for his skill, leadership, and courage. At the height of the attack, he led his line handling details to the quays, cast off the lines under fire, and then swam back to the ship. Later, while on the forecastle attempting to let go the anchors, he was blown overboard and killed by the explosion of several bombs. His performance of duty and devotion to duty was outstanding.[18]

A memorial for the USS *Nevada* is located directly behind the state capitol in Carson City, Nevada. The USS *Nevada* State Museum displays the ship's original sterling-silver service, uniforms, portions of her wooden deck, a large chest made in Nevada that contains Carson City–minted silver dollars presented to her crew during World War II, a model of the USS *Nevada*, and a photo collection.

The most famous and prominent memorial is located on Hospital Point in Oahu: a USS *Nevada* signboard and bronze tablet honoring the 50 *Nevada* crewmen killed and 105 injured during the Japanese attack of Pearl Harbor.[19]

In the *Cape May Star and Wave*, journalist Mark Allen wrote that Cape May's mayor, Zach Mullock, will have the necessary repairs done to Chief Boatswain Edwin Joseph Hill's memorial. His memorial will be moved to a place of honor at the All-Wars Memorial.[20]

The author visited Hill Walk and Chief Bos'n's memorial in Cape May October 2021. She noted the memorial is more visible, and the surroundings are more aesthetic. The memorial was not moved from its original spot.

Update January 24, 2022

Edwin Joseph Hill's new memorial, located in Hill Walk on the Washington Mall, Cape May, New Jersey. Photograph courtesy of Amy Furey.

After the attack, *Nevada* was temporarily repaired in Pearl Harbor. She then steamed on her own to Bremerton, Washington, for complete repairs and modernization.[21] The USS *Nevada* received a whole new superstructure. Author Paul Silverstone describes how *Nevada*'s tripod mainmast was removed and replaced with a smaller and lighter foremast. *Nevada*'s new profile was that of a pyramidal shape, which provided her with much greater fields of fire for the antiaircraft guns.[22] Both sides of the *Nevada* now carried four twin five-inch turrets. Radar was then fitted, and out of *Nevada*'s funnel, there now protruded a tall smoke tube.[23]

In 1943, the USS *Nevada* steamed north to the Aleutian Islands, providing support in the capture of Attu.[24] From Massacre Bay, the *Nevada* sailed south and through the Panama Canal to England for participation in the invasion of France in June 1944.[25] She fired upon the Germans, shattering Nazi gun emplacements, breaching the seawalls, destroying battery headquarters, and smashing German armored and motorized counterattacks.[26]

The website *Pearl Harbor in Hawaii* explains how the USS *Nevada* was chosen as the flagship for the Normandy invasion in 1944. The USS *Nevada* holds the distinction of being the only battleship present both during the Pearl Harbor attack and on D-Day.[27] During D-Day and Operation Dragoon, *Nevada* was highly praised for her precise firing capabilities and fortitude.[28]

In August 1944, the USS *Nevada* arrived off the Toulon and Marseilles areas, destroying Nazi shore batteries equipped with fifteen-inch guns from scuttled French battleships.[29] On September 25, 1944, the *Nevada* returned to the United States for maintenance in New York.[30]

The USS *Nevada* sailed back to the Pacific, participating in the invasion of Iwo Jima.[31] *Nevada*'s gunners drove Japanese defenders back into caves and foxholes, enabling the US Marine Corps to advance.

The USS *Nevada*'s final campaign took place during the invasion of Okinawa. On March 24, 1945, suicide planes and shore batteries attempted to destroy *Nevada*, but they were unsuccessful.[32] On March 27, 1945, a group of Japanese planes attacked the formation of fire-support ships. The *Nevada*'s antiaircraft gunners assisted in shooting down two Japanese planes. Suddenly, a Japanese Val dive-bomber streaked out of the hazy sky. *Nevada*'s guns blasted the plane apart.[38] Marine gunners in a twenty-millimeter battery sawed off the Val's right wing, which fluttered into the sea.[33] Loss of the wing diverted the aircraft's course from *Nevada*'s superstructure. However, the flaming plane then swerved and crashed into the main deck aft, alongside a main battery turret.[34]

The "*Ol Maru*," as *Nevada* was affectionately called by her crew, was still pounding away at Japanese airfields, shore defenses, and supply dumps and suspected Japanese troop concentration.[35] On April 5, a Japanese coastal battery unwisely sought to shoot at the *Nevada*. The engagement lasted eighteen minutes, but the experienced gunners on *Nevada* fired seventy-one rounds from the fourteen-inch main battery alone.[36] The Japanese battery was demolished.

The *Nevada* departed with the Third Fleet and sailed to a place off the Japanese coast. Word was received that the Japanese had asked for terms of surrender, and action was broken off.[37]

The USS *Nevada* returned to Pearl Harbor for an inspection and survey. It was determined the ship's age and past damages rendered her incapable of further warlike service expected of the modern navy.[38] The decorated battleship was decommissioned on August 29, 1946.[39] The USS *Nevada* was then selected to participate in Operations Crossroads, which would test the effects of an atomic bomb on US naval ships.[40] The *Nevada* sailed to Bikini Atoll in the Marshall Islands, where she was anchored along with other ships in the center of the nine-square-mile lagoon there.[41] *Nevada*'s decks were painted a bright orange to make her a more visible target for the air-dropped A-bomb.[42]

On June 30, 1946, a B-29 bomber from Kwajalein Atoll passed over the assembled ships at Bikini and dropped the missile.[43] A huge mushroom of water suddenly rose in the area. However, when the spray and smoke subsided, there stood the majestic *Nevada,* proving she could prevail even against the most destructive weapon ever invented.

The USS *Nevada* also bravely survived the underwater explosion connected with the tests. Later that year, she was towed back to Pearl Harbor.[44] An examination showed that while *Nevada* still floated, her sides and superstructure had been hopelessly damaged and buckled.[45]

In July 1948, the USS *Nevada* was painted orange to make her a more visible target, and she was towed sixty miles out to sea southwest of Pearl Harbor.[46] The navy placed a secret explosive aboard the battleship and detonated it.[47] *Nevada*'s side plates and deck buckled, and three holes opened up within the hull, but she remained afloat. The navy then decided to experiment with bat bombs, or radar-guided missiles.[48] However, the bombs failed to hit the *Nevada* and exploded six hundred yards astern.[49]

Next, the US Navy called upon some rocket-firing planes to end the USS *Nevada*'s agony.[50] The planes covered the ship's superstructure and hull with hundreds of gashes. Again, the USS *Nevada* refused to sink.[51] The USS *Iowa* (BB-61) was ten miles away from *Nevada,* and she fired sixteen-inch salvos against the battleship.[52] As the shells from *Iowa* hit *Nevada,* she became shrouded in smoke and spray. However, when a gentle breeze cleared the smoke, there remained the *Nevada,* with her decks still riding high above the Pacific's waves.[53] Next, three cruisers, the USS *Astoria* (CL-90), USS *Pasadena* (CL-65), and USS *Springfield* (CL-66), were called in to send *Nevada* to the bottom.[54] The three cruisers moved up and hammered away with their five- and six-inch guns, only to have *Nevada* remain in her defiant floating position.[55]

Navy dive-bombers were then called in and ordered to hit the USS *Nevada.*[56] During the afternoon of July 31, 1948, a flight of torpedo bombers attempted to sink the *Nevada.*[57] Shortly after 1400, a torpedo from one of the bombers caught the *Nevada* amidships, and she began listing slightly.[58] At 1434, the *Nevada* finally, suddenly capsized and sank stern first at latitude N 20°58′, longitude W 159°17′.[59]

The USS *Nevada* (BB-36) earned seven battle stars and other awards for multiple operations. She earned one star for each of the following:

- Pearl Harbor-Midway: December 7, 1941
- Aleutians Operations, Attu occupation: May 11–June 2, 1943
- Invasion of Normandy, including bombardment of Cherbourg: June 6–25, 1944
- Invasion of Southern France: August 15–September 25, 1944[60]

Today a ballistic missile submarine, the USS *Nevada* (SSBN-733), named after the great dreadnought, is based in Bangor, Washington.[61]

She was commissioned in 1986 and is a cornerstone of the US nuclear defense.[62]

The author noted the following article online in May 2020, on the website link following the article. She sent an email to James P. Delgado, PhD, RPA, asking if the following excerpt could be reprinted in this book.

Wreck of the Iconic Battleship USS *Nevada* Discovered in the Deep Pacific off Pearl Harbor

Good morning, everyone:

The news release has just gone out on our team and our partner's discovery of the wreck of USS *Nevada* (BB-36).

I believe that this discovery is timely. USS *Nevada* speaks to all of us, as Americans, to those of you who are also Nevadans, to all who served, who had or have family who serve, and in this difficult time, *Nevada* speaks to us from a watery grave to remind us of the indomitable spirit of the ship and her crew. In the dark days after December 7, 1941, *Nevada* was, while half sunk and on fire, a symbol of resolute determination, of service above self, and of our innate stubbornness as Americans to get up off the canvas and get back into the arena. USS *Hoga* and its crew rendered incredible service to *Nevada* that day. It was an honor years ago to author the study that made *HOGA* a National Historic Landmark. *Nevada* rose from the mud and water, and repaired and modernized, went on to fight in the Pacific and the Atlantic, shelling in support of the troops and other ships at D-Day, in the Aleutians, at Iwo and Okinawa. Hit by a kamikaze, shelled by Japanese shore batteries and taking more hits, and with more loss of life, *Nevada* persevered. BB-36 was the toughest ship in the Navy, and also defied two atomic bombs. It took nearly five days to sink her, and after that, USS *Iowa* sailed over the site and held a memorial service for USS *Nevada*. Never forgotten, she rests in three miles of water. It was a powerful moment as we guided the team driving a remotely operated vehicle three miles down as we sat in a control room 4,000 miles away and with a five-hour time difference to the stern and to see "36" as well as so many other reminders of the ship and crew.

Please feel free to share this release, and also note for any of you who wish to do statewide, local and historic, As one who met a number of Pearl Harbor veterans, including *Nevada* crew, and having the privilege to once interview Captain Donald K. Ross, who won the Medal of Honor that day for his actions on USS *Nevada*. I have wanted to find *Nevada* for a long time. The power of rediscovery, especially in the ocean deep, is wonderful to see. While never forgotten, the physical reality of the ship, broken and yet still largely intact, still painted, and sleeping in the dark will help connect this generation and time to USS *Nevada* and what she represents.

https://www.prnewswire.com/news-releases/uss-nevada-located-by-search-and-ocean-infinity-301056455.html

Respectfully,
Jim Delgado
James P. Delgado, PhD, RPA
SEARCH/SEARCH20
www.searchinc.com

APPENDIX

Our Lady Star of the Sea Chaplet Prayer

For Special Needs

Our Lady Star of the Sea, Stella Maris, is the patroness of the men who sail the seas. Saint Bonaventure reminds us that she also "guides to a landfall in heaven those who navigate the sea of this world in the ship of innocence or penance." Ships at sea might be guided by the North Star. Our Lady Star of the Sea not only aids the sailors aboard those ships but also aids all those who sail the stormy seas of life.

The Medal Prayer

A Prayer to the Blessed Virgin

Most beautiful Flower of Mount Carmel, Fruitful Vine, Splendor of Heaven, Blessed Mother of the Son of God, Immaculate Virgin, assist me in this my necessity. O, Star of the Sea, help me and show me herein that you are my Mother. Holy Mary, Mother of God, Queen of Heaven and Earth, I humbly beseech you from the bottom of my heart, to succor me in this necessity; there are none that can withstand your power.

First Three Beads:
Our Father, one Hail Mary, and one Glory Be.
On each of the three beads for Bishop Warren Boudreaux, Pope John Paul II and John Paul Finke.

On each of the 12 beads which represent the 12 stars on Our Lady's Crown, Pray:
One Hail Mary on each bead and the followed by the invocation:
Our Lady, Star of the Sea, help and protect us!
Sweet Mother, I place this cause in your hand.

+Imprimatur: Bishop Warren L. Boudreaux, Bishop of Houma, Thibodaux.

The Confraternity of Our Lady Star of the Sea in Morgan City, Louisiana, was established by Bishop Warren L. Boudreaux on August 22, 1979. Those wishing to obtain further information concerning membership may write: The Confraternity of Our Lady Star of the Sea, Central Headquarters, PO Box 609, Morgan City, LA 70381.

My Treasury of Chaplets Seventh, Enlarged Edition by Patricia S. Quintiliani.

GLOSSARY

aft: Near the stern (the end of the ship).

battleships: Ships that are heavily armored, carry heavy armament, and are of moderate speed, about twenty knots. They are designed to fight any vessel anywhere. All battleships have a large fuel capacity and a long cruising radius. Along with cruisers, battleships are divided into numerous watertight compartments.

bow: The forward end of the ship.

bridge: The raised platform extending athwartships in the forward part of the ship, from which the ship is steered and navigated. Amidships and after bridges are sometimes fitted.

bulwark: The planking or plating around the vessel above the upper deck.

capstan: A barrel of wood or steel turning around vertically on a central spindle. When forced to turn either by pushing on capstan bars or by steam, it serves to hoist heavy weights or to weigh anchor.

chief petty officer: An enlisted rank in the US Navy that is above petty officer first class and below senior chief petty officer.

commissioning: The act of placing a ship in commission marks her entry into active navy service. When the commissioning pennant is broken at the masthead, a ship becomes a navy command in her own right and takes her place alongside the other active ships of the fleet.

Congressional Medal of Honor: The Medal of Honor is the United States' highest award for military valor in action, honoring bravery, courage, sacrifice, integrity, a deep love of country, and a desire to always do what is right. The medal is authorized for any military service member who "distinguishes himself conspicuously by gallantry and intrepidity at the risk of his life above and beyond the call of duty:

- While engaged in an action against an enemy of the United States;
- While engaged in military operations involving conflict with an opposing foreign force; or
- While serving with friendly foreign forces engaged in an armed conflict against an opposing armed force in which the United States is not a belligerent party."

conning tower: The low, dome-shaped, armored pilothouse of a warship.

cruisers: Ships that are lightly armored, carry moderate armament, and are of high speed, about thirty-four knots. Ships with guns greater than six inches are known as heavy cruisers, while those with guns six inches or less are known as light cruisers. All cruisers have an extremely large fuel capacity to maintain a high speed for a long period of time.

decommissioning: To decommission a ship is to terminate its career in service in the armed forces of a nation. Unlike wartime ship losses, in which a vessel lost to enemy action is said to be struck, decommissioning confers that the ship has reached the end of its usable life and is being retired from a country's navy. Depending on the naval traditions of the country, a ceremony commemorating the decommissioning of the ship may take place, or the vessel may be removed administratively with minimal fanfare.

destroyer: A fast, relatively small warship armed mainly with five-inch (thirteen-centimeter) guns.

dreadnought: A type of battleship armed with heavy-caliber guns in turrets, named for the British battleship *Dreadnought,* launched in 1906, the first of its type.

forecastle: Portion of the ship that extends from the foremast forward on the uppermost deck.

galley: The cooking compartments on board a ship.

gangway: A narrow passage that joins the quarterdeck to the forecastle of a sailing ship. The term is also extended to the narrow passages used to board or disembark ships. Modern ships use gangways to embark and disembark passengers.

general quarters: Calls the ship's company to stations. General duties include the following: man the battery and take battle stations, load torpedoes, connect fire hose, stand by manifolds and valves, stand by cutout switches and switchboards, and test out all gear. Every officer and man must occupy his battle station at general quarters. Fleet working parties and ship's work and boating must give way to general quarters routine.

hull: The framework of the ship, providing structure.

Japanese Zero: Long-range-fire aircraft. The first two A6M1 prototypes were completed in March 1939, powered by the 580-kilowatt (780-horsepower) Mitsubishi Zuisei 13 engine with a two-blade propeller. It first flew on April 1, 1939, and passed testing within a remarkably short period. By September, it had already been accepted for navy testing as the A6M1 Type 0 carrier fighter, with the only notable change being a switch to a three-bladed propeller to cure a vibration problem.

keel: The lowest center-line longitudinal member. It is the first piece of metal laid on the blocks when building the ship.

magazine: A place where powder or shell is stowed.

midships: The middle portion of the ship.

minelayers: Specially designed ships for laying mines. They have moderate speed and carry a small battery. They carry special equipment for dropping mines over their sterns and are designed to carry anywhere from fifty to six hundred mines.

minesweepers: Small vessels specially equipped with cables for the sweeping of mines.

Navy Cross: A US Navy decoration awarded for outstanding heroism in operations against an enemy.

New York Ship Building: The New York Shipbuilding Corporation (or New York Ship for short) was an American shipbuilding company that operated from 1899 to 1968, ultimately completing more than five hundred vessels for the United States Navy, the United States Merchant Marine, the United States Coast Guard, and other maritime concerns.

Philadelphia Naval Yard: The Navy Yard, formerly known as the Philadelphia Naval Shipyard and Philadelphia Naval Business Center, was an important naval shipyard of the United States for almost two centuries. It is now a large mixed-use campus that employs nearly fifteen thousand people across a mix of industries and includes cutting-edge cell therapy production facilities, global fashion companies, and a commercial shipyard.

ports: Openings in the ship's side for various purposes. Air ports are for the admission of air and light. Gun ports are openings through which guns are pointed and fired.

port side: The left-hand side of the ship looking forward.

quarterdeck: The quarterdeck extends from the mainmast to the poop or to the stern if there is no poop.

radio compass: Used to determine the direction from which a radio wave comes.

rudder: The apparatus used to steer a vessel. It hangs on the sternpost, or rudderpost, by pintles and gudgeons.

ship departments: Each ship has the following departments: gunnery, navigation, engineer, construction and repair, supply, and medical. Each department is divided into divisions, based primarily on crews assigned to battle stations as follows:

gunnery: All gun, torpedo, and fire-control divisions, including the marines. Each gun division includes, as far as possible, only one class of gun.

navigation: Division for ship control and all communications control.

engineer: Main engine, boiler, auxiliary, and electrical divisions for ship propulsion.

construction and repair: Division for handling casualties to the ship.

supply: Cooks, bakers, and so on, stationed where they will be of greatest service.

medical: Division for treatment of personnel casualties.

The number of divisions on board the ship varies with the size of the ship and the number and caliber of the guns. The executive officer coordinates the work of the various heads of the departments and carries out the policies of the captain.[1391]

sortie: In siege warfare, a sortie, or sudden issuing of troops against the enemy from a defensive position, can be launched against the besiegers by the defenders. It is an armed attack, especially one made from a place surrounded by enemy forces. The term has been adopted from the French sortir, meaning "to leave" or "to go out" with a specific purpose.[1392]

sounding: Sounding is the act of determining the depth of water. Soundings may be taken with the hand lead, sounding machines, or the sonic depth finder.

starboard: The right-hand side of the ship looking forward.

stern: The after end of the ship.

strafing: To attack (ground troops or installations) by airplanes with machine-gun fire.

submarines: Specially designed ships that operate under the surface. For this purpose, they are fitted with ballast tanks, which, when flooded, cause the submarine to float with just a few hundred pounds' buoyancy. They are then submerged by going ahead with their electric motors and operating their diving rudders.

watertight compartment: All steel ships are divided into rooms and passages that are fitted to be watertight. Each separate compartment is known as a watertight compartment. The compartments serve to keep the ship afloat by confining the water if the hull is pierced.

wheel: The handwheel used to move the tiller and rudder. With the steam steering gear, the wheel, when turned, opens the valve of the steering engine, and the engine moves the rudder through a tiller or a crosshead. The wheel is connected to the valve by shafting and gearing, by a flexible wire cable, or, in some cases, by a telemotor (hydraulic piping system). The steam steering gear is not supplanted by electric and electric-hydraulic systems.

David B. Hill Jr.'s older brother William Langdon Hill, who served in the navy during World War II.

Deborah Fritz's grandfather Raymond Fischer, who served in the US Navy during World War I.

Deborah Fritz's father, William George Fischer, who served in the US Navy during World War II.

ACKNOWLEDGMENTS

First and foremost, thanks to God, our Lord and Savior, who guided us every step of this book. Thanks also to Mr. David B. Hill and his wife, Patria Garde-Hill; Chief Warrant Officer Edwin J. Hill's granddaughter, for sharing her firsthand experiences as well as invaluable information and photos; Mr. Ed Hill, Chief Boatswain Hill's nephew, for sharing his amazing photo collection and personal family information; Mr. William Furey and his wife, Amy, and Shannon Furey for their warm welcome and for sharing their wealth of information and encouragement; Commander Edwin Furey for his invaluable help, resources, and support and for writing the foreword; Edwin J. Hill's granddaughter Catherine "Cathy" Helen Roggeveen O'Connell, son Michael John Hill, granddaughter Patricia Marie Hill Tiegen for her invaluable source of information regarding her grandfather, grandson Steven John Hill, and grandson James Edwin Hill; and Mr. William Kelly, who gladly shared information from his exhaustive research. His blog provided treasures of information, including firsthand accounts.

Mr. Kelly interviewed Edwin J. Hill's daughter; his brother William Hill; Chief Warrant Officer (later Captain) Donald Ross; and Ensign Joseph (later Assistant Secretary to the US Navy) Taussig. Thanks to Emilee Brown, great-great-grandniece of Edwin J. Hill, for her encouragement, support, and enthusiasm as well as her connection to Peter Hill; Mr. Peter Hill, great-great-grandnephew of Edwin J. Hill, for sharing another photo of Chief Warrant Officer Edwin J. Hill standing at attention on the USS *Pennsylvania* and for connecting us to his father, James Hill; and Mr. James Hill, great-grandson of John Hill, brother of Chief Warrant Officer Edwin J. Hill, for information about John and Edwin Hill. Thanks to my husband, Warren; my daughter Sarah; and my daughter Kim for their ongoing encouragement, support, and help. Their proofreading has been invaluable. I thank Wendy and David Newdeck for their helpful proofreading and Rodrigo James Garde for his invaluable help in locating photos and documents. To all of Edwin J. Hill's family and descendants, may you be richly blessed. Thanks to Mark Allen for sharing his columns and information and for his enthusiasm and to the *Cape May Star and Wave* for permission to reprint their articles. Thanks to David B. Hill Jr.'s older brother William, who served in the navy during World War II. He made a far-reaching impact on the world during his short life. Thanks to my grandfather Raymond Fischer, who served in the US Navy during World War I, and my father, William George Fischer, who served in the US Navy during World War II. He was stationed in Hawaii after Pearl Harbor and sailed to Japan at the end of the war. Thank you to my editors. Thanks to all US military personnel—US Navy, US Marines, US Army, US Air Force, US Coast Guard, US National Guard, US Merchant Marines, and all Reserves—who fought on the Day of Infamy, December 7, 1941. Many offered themselves as living sacrifices for America's freedom. I want to also acknowledge all the civilians present that day in Pearl Harbor. At least sixty lost their lives, mostly due to friendly fire. Finally, thank you to all branches of the US military and auxiliary personnel for devoting their lives to the safety of the American public.

RECOMMENDED READING

1. http://www.navsource.org/archives/01/36a.htm. Excellent timeline of the USS *Nevada*.
2. *Tora! Tora! Tora!* Accurate film portraying both the American and the Japanese sides, starring Jason Robards, So Yamamura, and Martin Balsam. Originally released in 1970 by Twentieth-Century Fox. It won an Academy Award for Best Special Visual Effects. The DVD was released on May 23, 2006.
3. https://www.youtube.com/watch?v=SthNGbqzoy8. *Remembering Pearl Harbor (2001).* November 10, 2014.
4. Rogers, Keith. "Remembering the USS *Nevada*'s Daring Run for the Sea during Attack on Pearl Harbor." *Las Vegas Review-Journal*. December 5, 2016. https://www.reviewjournal.com/news/military/remembering-the-uss-nevadas-daring-run-for-the-sea-during-attack-on-pearl-harbor/.

5. https://www.reviewjournal.com/news/military/remembering-the-uss-nevadas-daring-run-for-the-sea-during-attack-on-pearl-harbor/. Excellent article and video about the USS *Nevada,* including Chief Boatswain Edwin Hill.
6. https://www.smithsonianmag.com/videos/category/history/the-only-live-news-report-from-the-attack-on_1/. "The Only Live News Report from the Attack on Pearl Harbor." On December 7, 1941, an NBC radio affiliate in Honolulu made an urgent phone call to New York. This phone call is the only known live report of Pearl Harbor.
7. http://nevadasortieatpearlharbor.blogspot.com/. William Kelly's blog.

NOTES

Chapter 1

1. Conversation with James Hill, June 2019.
2. Letter to John J. Hill III from William Hill, May 21, 1965, courtesy of William Furey, from his personal collection. Written permission to reprint this letter has been provided by Ed Hill.
3. Ibid.
4. Ibid.
5. Ibid.
6. Ibid.
7. Susan Tischler, "A Look at Early Victorian Architecture," CapeMay.com, September 1, 2006, https://www.capemay.com/blog/2006/09/a-look-at-early-victorian-architecture/.
8. Ibid.
9. Susan Tischler, "Cape May on Fire," CapeMay.com, November 1, 2003, https://www.capemay.com/blog/2003/11/cape-may-on-fire/.
10. Ibid.
11. Ibid.
12. Ibid.

13. Letter to John J. Hill III from William H. Hill, May 21, 1965, courtesy of William Furey, from his personal collection. Written permission to reprint this letter provided by Ed Hill.
14. Ibid.
15. Ibid.
16. Conversation with James Hill, April 2019.
17. Ibid.
18. Letter to John J. Hill III from William H. Hill, May 21, 1965, courtesy of William Furey, from his personal collection. Written permission to reprint this letter provided by Ed Hill.
19. Ibid.
20. Ibid.
21. Ibid.
22. Do the Shore, "A History of Cape May—Congress Hall and the Rusty Nail," February 20, 2013, http://dotheshore.com/dining/rusty-nail/history-cape-may-congress-hall-and-rusty-nail.
23. Bob Dreyfuss, "The Ghosts of Congress Hall," *Cape May Magazine*, June 2016, http://www.capemaymag.com/the-ghosts-of-congress-hall/.
24. Do the Shore.
25. Dreyfuss.
26. Ibid.
27. Do the Shore.
28. Jennifer Brownstone Kopp, "History, This Is Cape May, Congress Hall in 2002," CapeMay.com, June 1, 2002, https://www.capemay.com/blog/2002/06/congress-hall-in-2002/.
29. http://www.Ancestry.com.
30. Conversation with David Hill and Patria Garde-Hill, January 2019.
31. Ibid.
32. Ibid.
33. Ibid.
34. Ibid.
35. Ibid.
36. Ibid.

Chapter 2

1. William Kelly, "The Sortie of the USS *Nevada*," USS *Nevada* Sortie at Pearl Harbor, Tuesday, December 6, 2011, kellycombatheroes.blogspot.com, http://nevadasortieatpearlharbor.blogspot.com/. This is William Kelly's blog about Edwin Hill. It is very informative and recommended reading.
2. Ibid.
3. Ibid.
4. Ibid.
5. Ibid.
6. "The Salute Uniforms," US Navy Boatswain's Mate (BM) Rating Badge, http://www.uniforms-4u.com/p-navy-dress-blue-uniform-rating-badge-bm-1st-class-po-male-red-. http://www.Ancestry.comchevrons-3930.aspx.
7. Shilavadra Bhattacharjee, "Duties of a Bosun (Boatswain) on a Ship," Marine Insight, September 2, 2021, https://www.marineinsight.com/careers-2/duties-of-bosun-boatswain-on-a-ship/.
8. Ibid.
9. *Chron* contributor, "The Duties of a Boatswain," *Chron*, January 19, 2021, https://work.chron.com/duties-boatswain-20927.html.
10. Ibid.
11. Ibid.
12. http://www.Ancestry.com.
13. Ibid.
14. Ibid.
15. Ibid.
16. "Boatswain's Pipe Calls," Pipe Calls, Navy Menu, MilitaryWives.com.
17. Ibid.
18. "Chief Petty Officer Resource Links," CPO History and Traditions, Goat Locker, http://www,goatlocker.org/cpo-resources.html.
19. http://nevadasortieatpearlharbor.blogspot.com/.
20. Kyle Burns, Pennsylvania Center for the Book, USS *Pennsylvania*, 2010, http://pabook2.libraries.psu.edu/palitmap/USSPA.html.
21. Ibid.
22. Ibid.
23. Ibid.

24. Pennsylvania Military Museum, "USS *Pennsylvania* (BB-38)," Pennsylvania Historical and Museum Commission, https://www.pamilmuseum.org/uss-pennsylvania.
25. http://nevadasortieatpearlharbor.blogspot.com/.
26. Conversation with Patricia Tiegen, August 2020.
27. Conversation with Patricia Tiegen, August 2020.
28. "Naval History and Heritage Command," National Museum of the Navy, https://www.history.navy.mil/content/history/nhhc/search.html?q=uss+saratoga.
29. "USS *Saratoga*," *Wikipedia*, https://en.wikipedia.org/wiki/USS_Saratoga_(CV-3).
30. https://www.history.navy.mil/content/history/nhhc/search.html?q=uss+saratoga.
31. http://www.Ancestry.com.
32. "USNHistory.Navylive.Dolive.Mil," *Sextant*, "Navy History Matters," Thursday, January 1, 1970, https://usnhistory.navylive.dodlive.mil/2014/11/26/prelude-to-war-japanese-strike-force-takes-aim-at-pearl-harbor/.
33. Ibid.
34. Original letter written by Chief Boatswain Edwin J. Hill to his family in October 1941 while he was out to sea. Courtesy of William Furey, from his personal collection. Reprinted with permission from William Furey.

Chapter 3

1. Stephen M. Younger, *Silver State Dreadnought: The Remarkable Story of Battleship* Nevada (Annapolis, Maryland: Naval Institute Press, 2018), 131.
2. *History of Ships Named* Nevada 1, Navy Department Office of the Chief of Naval Operations Division of Naval History (OP 09B9), Ships' Histories Section.
3. *History of Ships Named* Nevada, 2.
4. Ibid.
5. Ibid.
6. Ibid.
7. Ibid.
8. Ibid.
9. Ibid.
10. Ibid.

11. Ibid.
12. Ibid.
13. Ibid.
14. Ibid.
15. Paul Silverstone, "A New Generation of Dreadnoughts," *Sea Classics* 22 (August 1989): 10–15.
16. Ibid.
17. Wayne Scarpaci, *Battleship* Nevada*: The Extraordinary Ship of Firsts*, 3rd ed. (Garnerville, NV: Art by Wayne, 2015).
18. *History of Ships Named* Nevada, 2.
19. *History of Ships Named* Nevada, 3.
20. Ibid.
21. Ibid.
22. Ibid.
23. Ibid.
24. Ibid.
25. Michael Slackman, *Remembering Pearl Harbor: The Story of the USS* Arizona *Memorial* (Honolulu, Hawaii: Arizona Memorial Museum Association).
26. Slackman, 11.
27. Slackman, 11.
28. Slackman, 11.
29. Roy Cook, "Pearl Harbor before Dec. 7, 1941, and Native Americans after Dec. 7, 1941," pdf. http://aiwa.americanindiansource.com/pearlharbor.html.
30. Slackman, 11.
31. http://aiwa.americanindiansource.com/pearlharbor.html.
32. Ibid.
33. Ibid.
34. Ibid.
35. Ibid.
36. Ibid.
37. Ibid.
38. Ibid.
39. https://visitpearlharbor.org/pearl-harbor-through-history-part-1/.
40. Slackman, 11.
41. Ibid.
42. http://aiwa.americanindiansource.com/pearlharbor.html.

43. Ibid.

44. Ibid.

45. Ibid.

46. https://usnhistory.navylive.dodlive.mil/2014/11/26/prelude-to-war-japanese-strike-force-takes-aim-at-pearl-harbor/.

47. Ibid.

48. Ibid.

49. Ibid.

50. Ibid.

51. Ibid.

52. Ibid.

53. https://usnhistory.navylive.dodlive.mil/2014/11/26/prelude-to-war-japanese-strike-force-takes-aim-at-pearl-harbor/.

54. Ibid.

55. Facts and Details. Asian Topics. "Japan Gears Up for World War II." http://factsanddetails.com/asian/ca67/sub427/item2535.html#chapter-3.

56. https://usnhistory.navylive.dodlive.mil/2014/11/26/prelude-to-war-japanese-strike-force-takes-aim-at-pearl-harbor/.

57. https://usnhistory.navylive.dodlive.mil/2014/11/26/prelude-to-war-japanese-strike-force-takes-aim-at-pearl-harbor/.

58. Ibid.

59. Ibid.

60. Ibid.

61. http://factsanddetails.com/asoam/ca67/sub427/item2535.html.

62. Keith Rogers, "Remembering the USS *Nevada*'s Daring Run for the Sea during Attack on Pearl Harbor," *Las Vegas Review Journal*, December 5, 2016, https://www.reviewjournal.com/news/military/remembering-the-uss-nevadas-daring-run-for-the-sea-during-attack-on-pearl/harbor.

63. David J. Rogers, American & Military History, "How One Man Can Change History," May 31, 2013, https://web.mst.edu/~rogersda/american&military history/Rogers-HowOneManCanChangeHistory-Minimum-May31-2013.pdf. This is an outstanding pdf. It is about CWO Donald Kirby Ross, but it has a lot of great information about Chief Boatswain Edwin Hill and the USS *Nevada*.

64. Mister Mac, TheLeanSubmariner: Steel Boats, Iron Men, and Their Stories (Plus a Bit More), "The Patten Family and the USS *Nevada*

(1941)," September 7, 2018, https://theleansubmariner.com/2018/09/07/the-patten-family-and-the-uss-nevada-1941/.

65. Ibid.
66. http://factsanddetails.com/asian/ca67/sub427/item2535.html.
67. https://web.mst.edu/~rpgersda/american&military_history/Rogers-HowOneManCanChangeHistory-Minimum-May31-2013.pdf.
68. Ibid.
69. https://ww2db.com/ship_spec.php?ship_id=315.
70. Ibid.
71. Ibid.
72. Mark J. Perry, "Lieutenant Survives the Pearl Harbor Attack aboard the USS *Nevada*," HistoryNet, January 1998, www.historynet.com/pearl-harbor-attack-lietenant-lawrence-ruff-survived-attack-aboard-uss-nevada.htm.
73. http://factsanddetails.com/asain/ca67/sub427/item2535.html.
74. Ibid.
75. Ibid.
76. Ibid.
77. Ibid.

Chapter 4

1. https://web.mst.edu/~rogersda/american&militaryhistory/Rogers-HowOneManCanChangeHistory-Minimum-May-2013.pdf p.18.
2. http://usnhistory.navylive.doddlive.mil/2014/12/04/navy-action-reports-tell-the-story-of-pearl-harbor-attack/.
3. Ibid.
4. Donald Stratton and Ken Gire, *All the Gallant Men: The First Memoir by a USS* Arizona *Survivor* (New York: HarperCollins, 2016), 78.
5. Younger, 131.
6. Ibid.
7. Stratton, 79; and http://factsanddetails.com/asian/ca67/sub427/item2535.html.
8. http://factsanddetails.com/asian/ca67/sub427/item2535.html.
9. https://web.mst.edu/~rogersda/american&military history/Rogers-HowOneManCanChangeHistory-Minimum-May31-2013.pdf.19.
10. http://factsanddetails.com/asian/ca67/sub427/item2535.html.
11. Ibid.

12. Ibid.
13. Ibid.
14. Ibid.
15. NavSource Naval History Photographic History of the US Navy, "Battleship Photo Archive," http://navsource.org/archives/01/pdf/014801x.pdf.
16. Ibid.
17. Ibid.
18. Ibid.
19. http://usnhistory.navylive.dodlive.mil/2014/12/04/navy-action-reports-tell-the-story-of-pearl-harbor-attack/.
20. Ibid.
21. Ibid.
22. Ibid.
23. Ibid.
24. Ibid.
25. Ibid.
26. Ibid.
27. http://factsanddetails.com/asian/ca67/sub427/item2535.html.
28. Prange, 505.
29. https://warfarehistorynetwork.com/daily/wwii/eye-witnesses-on-battleship-row/.
30. Ibid.
31. Ibid.
32. Stratton, 81.
33. https://web.mst.edu/~rogersda/american&militaryhistory/Rogers-HowOneManCanChangeHistory-Minimum-May31-2013. 1.
34. Frank Smitha, "The Attack at Pearl Harbor and the Philippines," Pearl Harbor and War in Southeast Asia, http://www.fsmitha.com/h2/ch22b4.htm.
35. Ibid.
36. Younger, 132.
37. Younger, 131–2.
38. Ibid.
39. Ibid.
40. Ibid.
41. http://usnhistory.navylive.dodlive.mil/2014/12/04/navy-action-reports-tell-the-story-of-pearl-harbor-attack/.
42. Ibid.

43. Ibid.

44. Prange, 505.

45. Ibid.

46. http://navsource.org/archives/01/pdf/014801xpdf.

47. Ibid.

48. Ibid.

49. https://warfarehistorynetwork.com/daily/wwii/eye-witnesses-on-battleship-row/.

50. www.historynet.com/pearl-harbor-attack-lieutenant-lawrence-ruff-survived-attack-aboard-uss-nevada.htm.

51. Ibid.

52. Ibid.

53. https://www.youtube.com/watch?v=A2Ujh9689D4. In a 2010 interview, Robert Welkner explained his role on the USS *Nevada* on the day of the attack. He unloaded the garbage onto a barge, which was pulled up next to the USS *Arizona*.

54. http://nevadasortieatpearlharbor.blogspot.com/.

55. Lieutenant J. K. Taussig, "My Crew at Pearl Harbor," *Coronet* 13, no. 6 (April 1943): 137–49.

56. Taussig, 139.

57. www.historynet.com/pearl-harbor-attack-lieutenant-lawrence-ruff-survived-attack-aboard-uss-nevada.htm.

58. Ibid.

59. Younger, 133.

60. Ibid.

61. https://warfarehistorynetwork.com/daily/wwii/eye-witnesses-on-battleship-row/.

62. Ibid.

63. Ibid.

64. https://factsanddetails.com/asian/ca67/sub427/item2535.html.

65. Ibid.

66. Ibid.

67. Ibid.

68. www.historynet.com/pearl-harbor-attack-lieutenant-lawrence-ruff-survived-attack-aboard-uss-nevada.htm.

69. Ibid.

Chapter 5

1. Wallace Louis Exum, *Battlewagon: Of the Nine Battleships at Pearl Harbor, One Got Underway* (New York: Vantage Press, 1974), 134. This book is a historical novel, but everything Exum writes is true and clear. It was helpful for me to refer to this book.
2. Charles Sehe, "Nevada Appeal," *Lahontan Valley News,* November 10, 2015, https://www.nevadaappeal.com/news/opinion/remembering-pearl-harbor-uss-nevada-a-spirited-ship/#; and http://nevadasortieatpearlharbor.blogspot.com/.
3. http://nevadasortieatpearlharbor.blogspot.com/.
4. Ibid.
5. Ibid.
6. Ibid.
7. Ibid.
8. Ibid.
9. http://usnhistory.navylive.dodlive.mil/2014/12/04/navy-action-reports-tell-the-story-of-pearl-harbor-attack/.
10. Ibid.
11. Prange, 505.
12. Younger, 133.
13. Prange, 506; interview with RADM William R. Furlong, November 16, 1962, log of Oglala, December 7, 1941, PHA, part 16, 2257; part 22, 594–95.
14. Younger, 133.
15. https://web.mst.edu/~rogersda/american&militaryhistory/Rogers-HowOneManCanChangeHistory-Minimum-May31-3013.pdf.
16. Ibid.
17. Ibid.
18. Younger, 131.
19. Ibid.
20. Prange, 515.
21. http://nevadasortieatpearlharbor.blogspot.com/.
22. Ibid.
23. Ibid.
24. Ibid.
25. David Holstead, "Museum Musings: Pearl Harbor Survivor Recalls the Day of Infamy," *Harrison Daily Times,* November 29, 2018, https://harrisondaily.com/

news/museum-musings-pearl-harbor-survivor-recalls-the-day-of-infamy/article e65d27e8-f355-11e8-8f94-3f53170e1d37.html.

26. Ibid.

27. Ibid.

28. Ibid.

29. http://nevadasortieatpearlharbor.blogspot.com/.

30. Ibid.

31. https://web.mst.edu/~rogersda/american&militaryhistory/Rogers-HowOneManCanChangeHistory-Minimum-May31-2013.pdf,14.

32. Ibid.

33. Younger, 134.

34. Ibid.

35. Ibid.

36. http://nevadasortieatpearlharbor.blogspot.com/.

37. Ibid.

38. https://web.mst.edu/~rogersda/american&militaryhistory/Rogers-HowOneManCanChangeHistory-Minimum-May31-2013.pdf.

39. Ibid.

40. https://www.nevadaappeal.com/news/opinion/remembering-pearl-harbor-uss-nevada-a-spirited-ship/#.

41. Ibid.

42. Ibid.

43. Ibid.

44. Ibid.

45. Younger, 134.

46. Ibid.

47. Ibid.

48. https://web.mst.edu/~rogersda/american&militaryhistory/Rogers-HowOneManCanChangeHistory-Minimum-May31-2013.pdf.

49. Stratton, 81; PHA, part 16.

50. http://www.fsmitha.com/h2/ch22b4.htm.

51. Ibid.

52. http://factsanddetails.com/asian/ca67/sub427/item2535.html.

53. http://www.fsmitha.com/h2/ch22b4.htm.

54. Ibid.

55. Younger, 131–2.

56. Ibid.
57. Ibid.
58. Prange, 505.
59. Ibid.
60. Ibid.
61. Ibid.
62. http://navsource.org/archives/01/pdf/014801x.
63. Younger, 136–7.
64. Ibid.
65. Younger, 136–7; and https://web.mst.edu/~rogersda/american&military history/Rogers-HowOneManCanChangeHistory-Minimum-May31-2013.pdf.
66. https://www.latimes.com/archives/la-xpm-1991-12-030wr0737-story.html.
67. https://www.nevadaappeal.com/news/opinion/remembering-pearl-harbor-uss-nevada-a-spirited-ship/#. This website features Charles Sehe.
68. Ibid.
69. Ibid.
70. https://www.ibiblio.org/hyperwar/USN/ships/logs/BB/bb36-Pearl.html.
71. Ibid.
72. http://nevadasortieatpearlharbor.blogspot.com/.
73. Ibid.
74. Ibid.
75. https://www.omaha.com/news/military/nebraska-s-pearl-harbor-survivors-recount-their-memories-of-dec/article74e23013-00467-5914-821e-63752338313a.html.
76. Ibid.
77. https://www.historynet.com/pearl-harbor-attack-lieutenant-lawrence-ruff-survived-attack-aboard-uss-nevada.html.
78. Ibid.
79. Nelson, 300; and Taussig, 145.
80. https://www.historynet.com/pearl-harbor-attack-lieutenant-lawrence-ruff-survived-attack-aboard-uss-nevada.html.
81. Taussig, 145.
82. Ibid.
83. https://www.latimes.com/archives/la-xpm-1991-12-03-wr-737-story.html.
84. https://madison.com/wsi/news/local/veterans-memories-of-pearl-harbor-attack-still-sting-years-later/article512204a-206d-11e1-ac38-0019bb2963d4.html.

85. Ibid.

86. Ibid.

87. Vicki Grayson, "Moment of Decision: PRC Elmer (Remle) Grayson, USMC, aboard the USS *Nevada*," http://www.ibiblio.org/phha/Elmer.html.

88. Lieutenant J. K. Taussig, "My Crew at Pearl Harbor," *Coronet* 13, no. 6 (April 1943):146.

89. Ibid.

90. Ibid.

91. Ibid.

92. http://nevadasortieatpearlharbor.blogspot.com/. William Kelly interviewed ENS Joseph Taussig.

93. Prange, 506; interview with RADM William R. Furlong, November 16, 1962, log of Oglala, December 7, 1941, PHA, part 16, 2257; part 22, 594–5.

94. Prange, 511; log of Nevada, December 7, 1941, statement by Lt. Ichiro Kitajima, October 18, 1950; letter from Captain Joseph K. Taussig Jr., January.

95. Sandy Fiedler, "Pearl Harbor Survivor—Texan Vic Lively," South Texas Towns and Cities, South Texas Plains, May 2001, accessed February 28, 2019, http://www.texasescapes.com/WorldWarII/PearlHarborSurvivorVic/VicLively1JapaneseAttack.htm.

96. www.historynet.com/pear-harbor-attack-lieutenant-lawrence-ruff-survived-attack-aboard-uss-nevada.

97. https://theleansubmariner.com/2018/09/07/the-patten-family-and-the-uss-nevada-1941/. The Patten family had seven brothers aboard the USS *Nevada* during the attack of Pearl Harbor.

98. Younger, 137.

99. https://ww2db.com/shipspec.php?shipid=100. Author Peter Chen wrote this in *World War II Database*.

100. Ibid.

101. Ibid.

102. Ibid.

103. Ibid.

104. Younger, 137.

105. http://www.badassoftheweek.com/edwinhill.html.

106. www.historynet.com/pearl-harbor-attack-lieutentant-lawrence-ruff-survived-attack-aboard-uss-nevada.htm.

107. Ibid.

108. Younger, 137.

109. Keith Rogers, "USS *Nevada* and Her Crew Honored Anew for Pearl Harbor Exploits," *Las Vegas-Review Journal*, December 9, 2016, accessed February 27, 2019, https://reviewjournal.com/news/military/uss-nevada-and-her-crew-honorored-anew-for-pearl-harbor-exploits/.

110. https://web.mst.edu/~rogersda/american&militaryhistory/Rogers-HowOneManCanChangeHistory-Minimum-May31-2013.pdf.

111. Ibid.

112. https://www.historynet.com/pearl-harbor-attack-lietenant-lawrence-ruff-survived-attack-aboard-uss-nevada.htm.

113. https://web.mst.edu/~rogersda/american&militaryhistory/Rogers-HowOneManCanChangeHistory-Minimum-May31-3013.

114. https://www.historynet.com/pearl-harbor-attack-lieutenant-lawrence-ruff-survived-attack-aboard-uss-nevada.htm.

115. Ibid.

116. https://web.mst.edu/~rogersda/american&militaryhistory/Rogers-HowOneManCanChangeHistory-Minimum-May31-2013.pdf,36,39.

117. Wallace Louis Exum, 147.

118. Ibid.

119. Ibid.

120. https://www.latimes.com/archives/la-xpm-1991-12-03-wr-737-story.html.

121. https://wwwlatimes.com/archives/la-xpm-1991-12-03-wr-737-story.html. This is from an interview with Ensign Joseph Taussig by the *Los Angeles Times*.

122. Ibid.

123. Lord, 132–3.

124. http://factsanddetails.com/asian/ca67/sub427/item2535.html.

Chapter 6

1. Younger, 138.
2. Ibid.
3. Lord, 135–6.
4. Ibid.
5. Exum, 150.
6. Ibid.
7. Younger, 139.

8. https://web.mst.edu/~rogersda/american&militaryhistory/Rogers-HowOneManCanChangeHistory-Minimum-May31-2013.pdf.
9. Ibid.
10. Nelson, 300.
11. http://nevadasortieatpearlharbor.blogspot.com/.
12. Ibid.
13. https://web.mst.edu/~rogersda/american&military history/Rogers-HowOneManCanChangeHistory-Minimum-May31-2013.pdf.
14. Nelson, 300–1.
15. William Brown, "First-Hand Accounts of December 7, 1941, in Pearl Harbor," faculty mentor Wade Dudley, East Carolina University, accessed February 26, 2019, https://uncw.edu/surf/explorations/documentations/brownwilliam.pdf. This project involved researching and writing a narrative combining the firsthand accounts of sailors in the United States Navy at Pearl Harbor, Hawaii, on December 7, 1941.
16. Ibid.
17. Ibid.
18. Younger, 140.
19. Ibid.
20. Ibid.
21. Ibid.
22. Ibid.
23. Ibid.
24. Ibid.
25. Ibid.
26. Ibid.
27. https://marines.togetherweserved.com/usmc/servlet/tws.webapp.WebApp?cmd=ShadowBoxProfile&type=Person&ID=180380.
28. https://web.mst.edu/~rogersda/american&military history/Rogers-HowOneManCanChangeHistory-Minimum-May31-2013.pdf.
29. Ibid.
30. Ibid.
31. https://www.nevadaappeal.com/news/opinion/remembering-pearl-harbor-uss-nevada-a-spirited-ship/#.
32. Ibid.
33. Ibid.

34. Ibid.
35. Ibid.
36. Exum, 145.
37. Ibid.
38. Ibid.
39. Ibid.
40. https://web.mst.edu/~rogersda/american&military_history/Rogers-HowOneManCanChangeHistory-Minimum-May31-2013.pdf.
41. Nelson, 301.
42. Taussig, 148.
43. Ibid.
44. Ibid.
45. Exum, 152–3.
46. http://nevadasortieatpearlharbor.blogspot.com/.
47. Exum, 151.
48. https://web.mst.edu/~rogersda/american&militaryhistory/Rogers-HowOneManCanChangeHistory-Minimum-May31-2013.pdf.
49. Stu Richardson, "Schuylkill County at Pearl Harbor December 7, 1941," Schuylkill County Military History, Thursday, December 6, 2012, Pennsylvaniahttps://schuylkillcountymilitaryhistory.blogspot.com/2012/12/schuylkillcounty-at-pearl-harbor.html.
50. http://nevadasortieatpearlharbor.blogspot.com/.
51. https://web.mst.edu/~rogersda/amercian&militaryhistory/Rogers-HowOneManCanChangeHistory-Minimum-May31-2013.pdf.
52. Ibid.
53. http://www.stonekettle.com/2007/12/remembering-december-7th.html.
54. Ibid.
55. Ibid.
56. http://www.stonekettle.com/2007/12/remembering-december-7th.html.
57. Ibid.
58. http://nevadasortieatpearlharbor.blogspot.com/. William Kelly's interview with then CWO Donald Ross.
59. Ibid.
60. Ibid. William Kelly's interview with ENS Joseph Taussig.
61. Ibid. William Kelly's interview with ENS Joseph Taussig.

62. http://www.hawaiireporter.com/a-hero-from-pennsylvania-chief-boatswain-edwin-joseph-hill-usn-1894-1941/.

63. https://www.thevintagenews.com/2017/04/11/us-navy-sailor-edwin-j-hills-insane-act-of-bravery-during-attack-on-pearl-harbor/?fbclid=IwAR3hp6eOrot2ccVu0osvA-vHvw4BPVs6AvMZqvAhIgfTwaZURV33tHGN7kk.

64. http://nevadasortieatpearlharbor.blogspot.com/.

65. Ibid.

66. Ibid. William Kelly's interview with Mr. Herndon, who served on the USS *Nevada* during Pearl Harbor.

67. Ibid. William Kelly's interview with Mr. William West, who served on the USS *Nevada* during Pearl Harbor.

68. Jim Wright, "Don't Just Embrace the Crazy, Sidle Up Next to It and Lick Its Ear," Stonekettle Station, December 7, 2007, accessed February 25, 2019, http://www.stonekettle.com/2007/12/remembering-december-7th.html.

69. Ibid.

70. Ibid.

71. http://nevadasortieatpearlharbor.blogspot.com/.

72. https://web.mst.edu/~rogersda/american&militaryhistory/Rogers-HowOneManCanChangeHistory-Minimum-May31-2013.pdf.

73. https://reviewjournal.com/news/military/remembering-the-uss-nevadas-daring-run-for-the-sea-during-attack-on-pearl-harbor/.

74. https://ww2db.com/shipspec.php?shipid=100.

75. Ibid.

76. www.historynet.com/pearl-harbor-attack-lieutenant-lawrence-ruff-survived-attack-aboard-uss-nevada.htm; and https://www.reviewjournal.com/news/military/remembering-the-uss-nevadas-daring-run-for-the-sea-during-attack-on-pearl-harbor.

77. Ibid.

78. https://ww2db.com/shipspec.php?shipid=100.

79. https://reviewjournal.com/news/military/remembering-the-ussnevadas-daring-run-for-the-sea-during-attack-on-pearl-harbor/.

80. https://www.pearlharboraviationmuseum.org/pearl-harbor-blog/the-nevadas-run/. By Ray Panko of Pearl Harbor Aviation.

81. https://www.historynet.com/pearl-harbor-attack-lieutenant-lawrence-ruff-survived-attack-aboard-uss-nevada.htm. Perry described this in the HistoryNet blog.

82. Ibid.

83. Ibid.
84. Ibid.
85. Ibid.
86. https://nationalinterest.org/bog/buzz/i-served-battleship-nevada-and-survived-pearl-harbor-30282. According to my research, Seaman Second Class Charles Sehe is the only one living who served on the USS *Nevada* during the attack on Pearl Harbor. I could not find anything to refute this.
87. Ibid.
88. Ibid.
89. http://nevadasortieatpearlharbor.blogspot.com.
90. Ibid.
91. Ibid.
92. Ibid.
93. https://web.mst.edu/~rogersda/american&militaryhistory/Rogers-HowOneManCanChangeHistory-Minimum-May-2013.pdf.
94. https://www.history.navy.mil/content/history/nhhc/research/library/online-reading-room/title-list-alphabetically/p/pearl-harbor-navy-medical-activities.html.

Epilogue

1. http://www.badassoftheweek.com/edwinhill.html.
2. https://visitpearlharbor.org/pearl-harbor-hero-edwin-hill/.
3. Ibid.
4. http://nevadasortieatpearlharbor.blogspot.com/.
5. Ibid.
6. http://hawaiireporter.com/a-hero-from-pennsylvania-chief-boatswain-edwin-joseph-hill-usn-1894-1941/.
7. https://usnhistory.navylive.dodlive.mil/2015/12/02/medal-of-honor-receipients-for-pearl-harbor-attack-dec-7-1941-part-iii/.
8. Conversation with Patricia Tiegen, Chief Boatswain Edwin Hill's granddaughter.
9. Cape May's Washington Street Mall walkway dedication honoring Chief Boatswain Edwin J. Hill at Hill Walk, August 12, 1971.
10. http://nevadasortieatpearlharbor.blogspot.com/.
11. http://www.spokesman.com/stories/2005/dec/17/historical-farragut/.
12. Ibid.

13. Ibid.
14. Ibid.
15. Ibid.
16. Ibid.
17. Ibid.
18. https://www.ibiblio.org/hyperwar/USN/ships/logs/BB/bb36-Pearl.html.
19. Conversation with Patricia Tiegen.
20. Mark Allen, "Hill Plaque to Be Returned to Place of Honor at Park," *Cape May Star and Wave,* February 10, 2021. Mr. Allen gave the author permission to reprint this from his article.
21. *History of Ships Named* Nevada, 10. This handy pamphlet was given to me by William Furey.
22. Silverstone, 15. This book is an outstanding reference about everything regarding the USS *Nevada.*
23. Ibid.
24. *History of Ships Named* Nevada, 10.
25. Ibid.
26. Ibid.
27. https://pearlharborinhawaii.com/ussnevada.html.
28. Ibid.
29. *History of Ships Named* Nevada, 11.
30. Ibid.
31. Ibid.
32. *History of Ships Named* Nevada, 12.
33. Ibid.
34. Ibid.
35. *History of Ships Named* Nevada, 13.
36. Ibid.
37. Ibid.
38. Ibid.
39. Ibid.
40. Ibid.
41. Ibid.
42. Ibid.
43. Ibid.
44. Ibid.

45. Ibid.

46. *History of Ships Named* Nevada, 14.

47. Ibid.

48. Ibid.

49. Ibid.

50. Ibid.

51. Ibid.

52. Ibid.

53. Ibid.

54. Ibid.

55. Ibid.

56. Ibid.

57. Ibid.

58. Ibid.

59. Ibid.

60. Ibid.

61. https://www.reviewjournal.com/news/military/remembering-the-uss-nevadas-daring-run-for-the-sea-during-attack-on-pearl-harbor/.

62. Ibid.

BIBLIOGRAPHY

"80-G-182252 Pearl Harbor Attack, 7 December 1941." Naval History and Heritage Command. Accessed January 8, 2019. https://www.history.navy.mil/content/history/nhhc/our-collections/photography/wars-and-events/world-war-ii/pearl-harbor-raid/japanese-forces-in-the-pearl-harbor-attack/miscellaneous-views-of-japanese-forces/80-G-182252.html.

"80-G-182259 Pearl Harbor Attack, 7 December 1941." Naval History and Heritage Command. Accessed January 8, 2019. https://www.history.navy.mil/content/history/nhhc/our-collections/photography/wars-and-events/world-war-ii/pearl-harbor-raid/japanese-forces-in-the-pearl-harbor-attack/miscellaneous-views-of-japanese-forces/80-G-182259.html.

"80-G-19940 Pearl Harbor Attack, 7 December 1941." Naval History and Heritage Command. Accessed January 5, 2019. https://www.history.navy.mil/content/history/nhhc/our-collections/photography/us-navy-ships/battleships/nevada-bb-36/80-G-19940.html.

"80-G-19951 Pearl Harbor Attack, 7 December 1941." Naval History and Heritage Command. Accessed January 4, 2019. https://www.history.navy.mil/our-collections/photography/wars-and-events/world-war-ii/pearl-harbor-raid/battleship-row-during-the-pearl-harbor-attack/general-views/80-G-19951.html.

"80-G-279370 Pearl Harbor, Oahu, Hawaii." Naval History and Heritage Command. Accessed January 4, 2019. https://www.history.navy.mil/our-collections/photography/wars-and-events/world-war-ii/pearl-harbor-raid/pearl-harbor-in-1940-1941/80-G-279370.html.

"80-G-279385 Pearl Harbor, Oahu, Hawaii." Naval History and Heritage Command. Accessed January 4, 2019. https://www.history.navy.mil/our-collections/photography/wars-and-events/world-war-ii/pearl-harbor-raid/pearl-harbor-in-1940-1941/80-G-279385.html.

"80-G-32443 Pearl Harbor Attack, 7 December 1941." Naval History and Heritage Command. Accessed January 3, 2019. https://www.history.navy.mil/our-collections/photography/wars-and-events/world-war-ii/pearl-harbor-raid/battleship-row-during-the-pearl-harbor-attack/uss-nevada-during-the-pearl-harbor-attack/80-G-32443.html.

"80-G-32445 Pearl Harbor Attack, 7 December 1941." Naval History and Heritage Command. Accessed January 5, 2019. https://www.history.navy.mil/content/history/nhhc/our-collections/photography/wars-and-events/world-war-ii/pearl-harbor-raid/battleship-row-during-the-pearl-harbor-attack/uss-nevada-during-the-pearl-harbor-attack/80-G-32445.html.

"80-G-32457 Pearl Harbor Attack, 7 December 1941." Naval History and Heritage Command. Accessed January 5, 2019. https://www.history.

navy.mil/content/history/nhhc/our-collections/photography/wars-and-events/world-war-ii/pearl-harbor-raid/attacks-in-the-navy-yard-area/uss-shaw-during-the-pearl-harbor-attack/80-G-32457.html.

"80-G-32792 Pearl Harbor Attack, 7 December 1941." Naval History and Heritage Command. Accessed January 4, 2019. https://www.history.navy.mil/our-collections/photography/wars-and-events/world-war-ii/pearl-harbor-raid/overall-views-of-the-pearl-harbor-attack/80-G-32792.html.

"80-G-32894 Pearl Harbor Attack, 7 December 1941." Naval History and Heritage Command. Accessed January 3, 2019. https://www.history.navy.mil/our-collections/photography/wars-and-events/world-war-ii/pearl-harbor-raid/battleship-row-during-the-pearl-harbor-attack/uss-nevada-during-the-pearl-harbor-attack/80-G-32894.html.

"80-G-32894 Pearl Harbor Attack, 7 December 1941." Naval History and Heritage Command. Accessed January 5, 2019. https://www.history.navy.mil/content/history/nhhc/our-collections/photography/wars-and-events/world-war-ii/pearl-harbor-raid/battleship-row-during-the-pearl-harbor-attack/uss-nevada-during-the-pearl-harbor-attack/80-G-32894.html.

"80-G-33020 Pearl Harbor Attack, 7 December 1941." Naval History and Heritage Command. Accessed January 3, 2019. https://www.history.navy.mil/our-collections/photography/wars-and-events/world-war-ii/pearl-harbor-raid/battleship-row-during-the-pearl-harbor-attack/uss-nevada-during-the-pearl-harbor-attack/80-g-33020-pearl-harbor-attack.html.

"80-G-33035 Pearl Harbor Attack, 7 December 1941." Naval History and Heritage Command. Accessed January 4, 2019. https://www.history.navy.mil/our-collections/photography/wars-and-events/world-war-ii/

pearl-harbor-raid/battleship-row-during-the-pearl-harbor-attack/general-views/80-G-33035.html.

"80-G-33045 Pearl Harbor Attack, 7 December 1941." Naval History and Heritage Command. Accessed January 3, 2019. https://www.history.navy.mil/our-collections/photography/wars-and-events/world-war-ii/pearl-harbor-raid/overall-views-of-the-pearl-harbor-attack/80-G-33045.html.

"80-G-40056 Pearl Harbor Attack, 7 December 1941." Naval History and Heritage Command. Accessed January 3, 2019. https://www.history.navy.mil/our-collections/photography/wars-and-events/world-war-ii/pearl-harbor-raid/overall-views-of-the-pearl-harbor-attack/80-G-40056.html.

"80-G-411119 Pearl Harbor, Oahu, Hawaii." Naval History and Heritage Command. Accessed January 4, 2019. https://www.history.navy.mil/our-collections/photography/wars-and-events/world-war-ii/pearl-harbor-raid/pearl-harbor-in-1940-1941/80-G-411119.html.

"80-G-411136 USS *Melville*." Naval History and Heritage Command. Accessed January 7, 2019. https://www.history.navy.mil/content/history/nhhc/our-collections/photography/numerical-list-of-images/nara-series/80-g/80-G-410000/80-G-411136.html.

"80-G-71198 Pearl Harbor Attack, 7 December 1941." Naval History and Heritage Command. Accessed January 8, 2019. https://www.history.navy.mil/content/history/nhhc/our-collections/photography/wars-and-events/world-war-ii/pearl-harbor-raid/japanese-forces-in-the-pearl-harbor-attack/miscellaneous-views-of-japanese-forces/80-G-71198.html.

"About Cape May." City of Cape May. 2016. Accessed April 12, 2019. http://www.capemaycity.com/Cit-e-Access/webpage.cfm?TID=103&TPID=10602.

Avedissian, Susan. *Cape May Star and Wave*, December 7, 2001.

"A Hero from Pennsylvania? Chief Boatswain Edwin Joseph Hill, USN (1894–1941)." *Hawaii Reporter*, November 15, 2010. Accessed January 24, 2019. http://www.hawaiireporter.com/a-hero-from-pennsylvania-chief-boatswain-edwin-joseph-hill-usn-1894-1941/.

"A History of Cape May—Congress Hall and the Rusty Nail." DoTheShore.com. February 20, 2013. Accessed April 22, 2019. http://dotheshore.com/dining/rusty-nail/history-cape-may-congress-hall-and-rusty-nail.

"Aichi D3A." *Wikipedia*. January 7, 2019. Accessed February 25, 2019. https://en.wikipedia.org/wiki/Aichi_D3A.

Allen, Mark. "Hill Plaque to Be Returned to Place of Honor at Park." *Cape May Star and Wave*, February 10, 2021.

Allen, Mark. "Remembering Cape May's Pearl Harbor Battle Hero." *Cape May Star and Wave*, February 10, 2021.

Ancestry. Accessed January 3, 2019. https://www.ancestry.com/search/?name=Edwin J_Hill&gender=m&keyword=Pearl Harbor&name_x=_1.

Ancestry. Accessed January 6, 2019. https://www.ancestry.com/mediauiiewer/tree/16642405/person/272045097664/media/0946b3e2-ba96-4632-bbd7-463e3b301927?destTreeId=157261159&destPersonId=172068322022&_phsrc=wHl648&_phstart=default.

Ancestry. Accessed January 19, 2019. https://www.ancestry.com/family-tree/tree/157136261/family.

Amazon. 2016. Accessed January 10, 2019. https://www.amazon.com/Remember-Pearl-Harbor-Narrated-Selleck/dp/B01MXXKA95/ref=sr_1_1?s=instant-video&ie=UTF8&qid=1547087493&sr=1-1&keywords=pearl harbor documentary.

"A Sunday in December: Chapter 3: Hell in the Harbor." *Los Angeles Times*, December 3, 1991. Accessed April 4, 2019. https://www.latimes.com/archives/la-xpm-1991-12-03-wr-737-story.html.

"Attack on Pearl Harbor Pictures." History Link 101. Accessed February 24, 2019. Royalty Free Photos of Pearl Harbor. http://historylink101.com/wwII_b-w/pearl_harbor/index.html

"Badass of the Week: Ching Shih." Accessed January 24, 2019. http://www.badassoftheweek.com/edwinhill.html.

Bhattacharjee, Shilavadra. "Duties of a Bosun (Boatswain) on a Ship." Marine Insight. September 2, 2021. https://www.marineinsight.com/careers-2/duties-of-bosun-boatswain-on-a-ship/.

The Bluejackets' Manual, United States Navy. 10th ed. Annapolis, Maryland: United States Naval Institute, 1940.

"Boatswain." *Wikipedia.* December 6, 2018. Accessed January 4, 2019. https://en.wikipedia.org/wiki/Boatswain.

"Boatswain's Pipe Calls." Pipe Calls. Navy Menu. MilitaryWives.com.

Brown, William. "First-Hand Accounts of December 7, 1941, in Pearl Harbor." Accessed February 26, 2019. Faculty mentor Wade Dudley. East Carolina University. This project involved researching and writing a narrative combining the firsthand accounts of sailors in the United States

Navy at Pearl Harbor, Hawaii, on December 7, 1941. https://uncw.edu/csurf/Explorations/documents/BrownWilliam.pdf.

Burns, Kyle. Pennsylvania Center for the Book. USS *Pennsylvania*. 2010. Accessed April 19, 2019. http://pabook2.libraries.psu.edu/palitmap/USSPA.html.

"Camden, New Jersey." *Wikipedia*. January 13, 2019. Accessed January 21, 2019. https://en.wikipedia.org/wiki/Camden,_New_Jersey.

Campbell, Matt. "KC Area Observance Marks 75th Anniversary of Pearl Harbor Attack." *Kansascity*, December 7, 2016. Accessed March 27, 2019. https://www.kansascity.com/news/local/article119500533.html.

"Cape Curiosity." Exit Zero. Cape May, New Jersey. Accessed March 3, 2019. http://exitzero.us/2010/07/cape-curiosity-5/.

"Cape May Diamonds." *Wikipedia*. March 14, 2018. Accessed January 20, 2019. https://en.wikipedia.org/wiki/Cape_May_diamonds.

"Cape May Historic District." *Wikipedia*. November 8, 2018. Accessed January 7, 2019. https://en.wikipedia.org/wiki/Cape_May_Historic_District#/media/File:Congress_Hotel_CMHD.JPG.

"Cape May-Lewes Ferry History." Cape May-Lewes Ferry. June 20, 2018. Accessed January 7, 2019. https://www.cmlf.com/cape-may-lewes-ferry-history.

"Cape May, New Jersey." *Wikipedia*. December 19, 2018. Accessed January 7, 2019. https://en.wikipedia.org/wiki/Cape_May,_New_Jersey.

Cape May's Washington Street Mall walkway dedication honoring Chief Boatswain Edwin J. Hill at Hill Walk, August 12, 1971.

Chamberlin, Cain. "Cape May's Hill, a Pearl Harbor Hero." *Cape May Star and Wave*, December 7, 2011. Accessed February 25, 2019. http://www.starandwave.com/CMA 12-7-11 Page 1.pdf.

Chasten, M. A. New Jersey Intracoastal Waterway. March 13, 2020. Retrieved July 4, 2020. https://www.nap.usace.army.mil/Missions/Factsheets/Fact-Sheet-Article-View/Article/490826/new-jersey-intracoastal-waterway/.

Chen, Peter C., Alan Chanter, and David Stubblebine. "Battleship USS *Nevada* (BB-36)." WW2DB. Accessed January 25, 2019. https://ww2db.com/ship_spec.php?ship_id=100.

"Chief Boatswain Edwin J. Hill, USN (1894–1941)." Online Library of Selected Images. December 7, 2007. Accessed December 28, 2019. http://www.freerepublic.com/focus/f-news/1936025/posts.

"Chief Petty Officer Resource Links." CPO History and Traditions. Goat Locker. http://www.goatlocker.org/cpo-resources.html.

"Chief Petty Officer (United States)." *Wikipedia*. January 22, 2019. Accessed January 27, 2019. https://en.wikipedia.org/wiki/Chief_petty_officer_(United_States).

Chron contributor. "The Duties of a Boatswain." *Chron*, January 19, 2021. https://work.chron.com/duties-boatswain-20927.html.

"Chronology of the Attack from the Deck Logs of the Vessels Moored at Pearl Harbor December 7, 1941." NavSource Naval History. Compiled for the Pearl Harbor Court of Inquiry Hearings. Last revised October 2003. Accessed March 1, 2019. http://www.navsource.org/Naval/logs.htm.

"Citation Machine, a Chegg Service." *Citation Machine: Modern Language Association 8th Edition Format Citation Generator for Journal Article.* Accessed January 9, 2019. https://www.citationmachine.net/chicago/cite-a-website.

Citino, Robert. "Launching the War? Hirohito and Pearl Harbor." National WWII Museum. New Orleans. December 5, 2018. Accessed January 4, 2019. https://www.nationalww2museum.org/war/articles/launching-war-hirohito-and-pearl-harbor.

Clifton, Guy. "*Nevada*'s Namesake Battleship Celebrates 100 Years." *Reno Gazette Journal,* July 12, 2014. Accessed February 20, 2019. https://www.rgj.com/story/news/2014/07/11/nevadas-namesake-battleship-celebrate-years/12551147/.

Cole, William, and Honolulu Star-Advertiser. "For the First Time in Years, Pearl Harbor Remembrance Won't Have Any USS *Arizona* Survivors." *Task and Purpose,* December 28, 2018. Accessed February 28, 2019. https://taskandpurpose.com/pearl-harbor-remembrance-uss-arizona-survivors.

"Complete Version of 'The Star-Spangled Banner' Showing Spelling and Punctuation from Francis Scott Key's Manuscript in the Maryland Historical Society Collection." Accessed March 15, 2019. https://amhistory.si.edu/starspangledbanner/pdf/ssb_lyrics.pdf.

Cook, Roy. "Pearl Harbor before Dec. 7, 1941, and Native Americans after Dec. 7, 1941." *Pearl Harbor.* Accessed April 20, 2019. http://aiwa.americanindiansource.com/pearlharbor.html.

Crosby, Donald F. "Catholic Chaplains under Fire: Pearl Harbor a Half-Century Later." *Crisis Magazine,* July 15, 2013. Accessed January 8, 2019. At the time this article was published, Donald F. Crosby, SJ, lived at the University of San Francisco. He was completing work on a book about the Catholic chaplains of World War II: *Men of God, Men at War*. He passed away in 2002. https://www.crisismagazine.com/1992/catholic-chaplains-under-fire-pearl-harbor-a-half-century-later.

Crucibleteachnotes.html. Accessed January 3, 2019. https://www.ibiblio.org/hyperwar/USN/USN-Chron/USN-Chron-1941.html.

"Digital Collections: Street Atlas of Philadelphia by Wards, 32nd Ward." Free Library of Philadelphia. Accessed January 9, 2019. https://libwww.freelibrary.org/digital/item/16785.

Do the Shore. "A History of Cape May—Congress Hall and the Rusty Nail." February 20, 2013. http://dotheshore.com/dining/rusty-nail/history-cape-may-congress-hall-and-rusty-nail.

Documentaries, BBC Radio. YouTube. July 9, 2016. Accessed June 2019. https://www.youtube.com/watch?v=UjBWYlmrAks.

Dreyfuss, Bob. "The Ghosts of Congress Hall." *Cape May Magazine*, June 2016. http://www.capemaymag.com/the-ghosts-of-congress-hall/.

Dulle, Brian. "Kansas City Area's Last Pearl Harbor Survivor Has Died at 96." FOX 4 Kansas City WDAF-TV. March 19, 2019. Accessed March 27, 2019. https://fox4kc.com/2019/03/19/kansas-city-areas-last-pearl-harbor-survivor-has-died-at-96/.

"Edwin J. Hill." *Wikipedia*. November 8, 2018. Accessed January 24, 2019. https://en.wikipedia.org/wiki/Edwin_J._Hill.

"Edwin Joseph Hill." Medal of Honor. Congressional Medal of Honor Foundation. Accessed January 8, 2019. https://

themedalofhonor.com/medal-of-honor-recipients/recipients/hill-edwin-world-war-wo?fbclid=IwAR2hQwTcZn6XpNCwS_NiOjrx29cWJAMRhfiuerTX16VSPQQw08NWayBmgAo.

Erickson, Ruth. Excerpt from "Oral History of LT Ruth Erickson, NC (Nurse Corps), USN." Lieutenant Erickson was a nurse at Naval Hospital Pearl Harbor during the attack on December 7, 1941. Oral history provided courtesy of Historian, Bureau of Medicine and Surgery. https://www.history.navy.mil/content/history/nhhc/research/library/oral- histories/wwii/pearl-harbor/pearl-harbor-attack-lt-erickson.html.

Exum, Wallace Louis. *Battlewagon: Of the Nine Battleships at Pearl Harbor, One Got Underway.* New York: Vantage Press, 1974.

"Eyewitness to History Remembers the Attack on Pearl Harbor." The Christian Broadcasting Network. March 26, 2018. Accessed February 26, 2019. https://www1.cbn.com/video/lt-jim-downing-remembering-pearl-harbor.

Facts and Details. Asian Topics. "Japan Gears Up for World War II." http://factsanddetails.com/asian/ca67/sub427/item2535.html#chapter-3.

Fagart, Tom. "Fort Fisher to Elmira to Pearl Harbor." Elmira Prison Camp. August 28, 2016. Accessed March 12, 2019. http://www.elmiraprisoncamp.com/fort-fisher-to-elmira-to-pearl-harbor/.

Ferdinando, Lisa. "Pearl Harbor Survivors Honor Fallen USS *Nevada* Crew." US Department of Defense. December 9, 2016. Accessed February 19, 2019. https://dod.defense.gov/News/Article/Article/1026052/pearl-harbor-survivors-honor-fallen-uss-nevada-crew/.

Fiedler, Sandy. "Pearl Harbor Survivor—Texan Vic Lively." South Texas Towns and Cities, South Texas Plains. May 2001. Accessed February 28, 2019. http://www.texasescapes.com/WorldWarII/PearlHarborSurvivorVic/VicLively1JapaneseAttack.htm.

Find A Grave. Accessed January 27, 2019. https://www.findagrave.com/memorial/887452/herman-joseph-kossler.

"Fireman (steam engine)." *Wikipedia*. January 15, 2019. Accessed February 9, 2019. https://en.wikipedia.org/wiki/Fireman_(steam_engine).

"First-Hand Account of LT Ruth Erickson, NC (Nurse Corps), USN Assigned to Naval Hospital Pearl Harbor." Liberty Letters. 2006. Accessed February 27, 2019. http://www.libertyletters.com/resources/pearl-harbor/account-of-pearl-harbor.php.

Flagg, James Montgomery. "United States Navy Operations during World War I." *Wikipedia*. December 27, 2018. Accessed January 4, 2019. https://en.wikipedia.org/wiki/United_States_Navy_operations_during_World_War_I#/media/File:FlaggDontReadHistoryMakeIt.jpg.

Flight Tribute. YouTube. November 12, 2015. Accessed February 20, 2019. https://www.youtube.com/watch?v=Io038KRcw1I&t=170s.

Foley, Beth. "Pearl Harbor Survivor Recalls Historic Attack on US." *Palestine Herald*, December 7, 2008. Accessed February 28, 2019. https://www.palestineherald.com/news/pearl-harbor-survivor-recalls-historic-attack-on-u-s/article_fc02cc2d-df52-5396-b404-bb81572e9c35.html.

"Francis Thomas—Recipient." Military Times Hall of Valor. 2019. Accessed April 4, 2019. https://valor.militarytimes.com/hero/21024.

"Full History." Battleship New Jersey. Accessed April 23, 2019. https://www.battleshipnewjersey.org/the-ship/full-history"/.

Gannon, Michael. *Pearl Harbor Betrayed: The True Story of a Man and a Nation under Attack*. New York: Henry Holt and Company, 2001.

Gawron, James. "The Captain of the *Nevada*: Dec. 7, 1941." Ricochet. December 8, 2018. Accessed March 12, 2019. https://ricochet.com/578287/the-captain-of-the-nevada-dec-7-1941/.

"The Ghosts of Congress Hall." *Cape May Magazine*, December 2, 2016. Accessed March 3, 2019. http://www.capemaymag.com/the-ghosts-of-congress-hall/.

Gidlund, Carl. "Historical Farragut." Spokesman.com. June 30, 2009. Accessed February 26, 2019. http://www.spokesman.com/stories/2005/dec/17/historical-farragut/.

Gillette, Howard, Jr. "Camden, New Jersey." *Encyclopedia of Greater Philadelphia*. 2016. Accessed April 23, 2019. Howard Gillette Jr. is professor emeritus of history at Rutgers-Camden and author of *Camden after the Fall: Decline and Renewal in a Postindustrial City*. He is coeditor of *The Encyclopedia of Greater Philadelphia*. https://philadelphiaencyclopedia.org/archive/camden-new-jersey/.

Grayson, Vicki. "Moment of Decision: PRC Elmer (Remle) Grayson, USMC, aboard the USS *Nevada*." http://www.ibiblio.org/phha/Elmer.html.

The Great War. YouTube. November 24, 2014. Accessed January 26, 2019. https://www.youtube.com/watch?v=P92guhd7d-8.

Griffith, John. Find A Grave. Accessed January 3, 2019. https://www.findagrave.com/memorial/7749155/edwin-joseph-hill.

"H-001-3 Valor." Naval History and Heritage Command. October 20, 2017. Accessed January 5, 2019. https://www.history.navy.mil/content/history/nhhc/about-us/leadership/director/directors-corner/h-grams/h-gram-001/h-001-3.html.

Halpern, Paul. "The US Navy in the Great War." Trenches on the Web—Special. Accessed January 6, 2019. http://www.worldwar1.com/tgws/usnwwone.htm.

Hays, Jeffrey. "Pearl Harbor and Eyewitness Accounts of the Attack." Facts and Details. Accessed January 3, 2019. http://factsanddetails.com/asian/ca67/sub427/item2535.html.

"Herman Kossler—Recipient." Military Times Hall of Valor. Sightline Media Group. Accessed January 27, 2019. https://testvalor.militarytimes.com/hero/20609

"Hill-Chase and Company Photographs." October 20, 2015. Accessed February 22, 2019. http://dla.library.upenn.edu/cocoon/dla/pacscl/ead.pdf?id=PACSCL_HML_2006238.

Creator: Hill Chase & Company circa 1945–1951, bulk 1945-1951Call number 238.

Historical Society, Kansas. "World War I Navy Uniform." Kansas Historical Society. Last modified July 2017. Accessed January 26, 2019. https://www.kshs.org/kansapedia/world-war-i-navy-uniform/17284.

"History." Old Saint Joseph's Church. Accessed April 11, 2019. Acknowledgement and thanks to Martin I. J. Griffin, M. Maury Walton, Eugene Gallagher, SJ, and John M. Daley, SJ, for essays and pamphlet histories of Old St. Joseph's. https://oldstjoseph.org/about-osj/history/.

"History." Naval History and Heritage Command. Accessed January 25, 2019. https://www.history.navy.mil/browse-by-topic/wars-conflicts-and-operations/world-war-i/history.html.

"History of Our Lady Star of the Sea Church." Accessed February 22, 2019. http://www.ladystarofthesea.org/olss/History of Our Lady Star of the Sea Church.pdf?1528316159.

History of Ships Named Nevada. Navy Department Office of the Chief of Naval Operations Division of Naval History (OP 09B9), Ships' Histories Section.

"History of Warrant Officers in the US Navy." Naval History and Heritage Command. Accessed February 22, 2019. https://www.history.navy.mil/research/library/online-reading-room/title-list-alphabetically/w/naval-traditions-names-of-rank/history-of-warrant-officers-in-the-us-navy.html.

Holsted, David. "Museum Musings: Pearl Harbor Survivor Recalls the Day of Infamy." *Harrison Daily*, November 29, 2018. Accessed February 25, 2019. This article is part of a series about Boone County history and provided by the Boone County Heritage Museum. http://harrisondaily.com/news/museum-musings-pearl-harbor-survivor-recalls-the-day-of-infamy/article_e65d27e8-f355-11e8-8f94-3f53170e1d37.html.

"Husband E. Kimmel." *Wikipedia*. February 28, 2019. Accessed March 15, 2019. https://en.wikipedia.org/wiki/Husband_E._Kimmel.

"Idaho2." Medal of Honor Historical Society of the United States. Accessed January 3, 2019. http://www.mohhsus.com/idaho2.

"In Memoriam: Pearl Harbor Survivors We Lost in 2017." Visit Pearl Harbor. January 5, 2018. Accessed February 28, 2019. https://visitpearlharbor.org/memoriam-pearl-harbor-survivors-lost-2017/.

"Ireland and World War I." *Wikipedia*. December 13, 2018. Accessed January 6, 2019. https://en.wikipedia.org/wiki/Ireland_and_World_War_I.

"Irish Blessings and Prayers." Island Ireland: Irish Blessings and Prayers. Accessed April 22, 2019. http://www.islandireland.com/Pages/folk/sets/bless.html.

"Isaac C. Kidd." *Wikipedia*. November 9, 2018. Accessed February 25, 2019. https://en.wikipedia.org/wiki/Isaac_C._Kidd.

"Japanese Aircraft during and after the Raid." Naval History and Heritage Command. Accessed January 21, 2019. https://www.history.navy.mil/content/history/nhhc/our-collections/photography/wars-and-events/world-war-ii/pearl-harbor-raid/japanese-forces-in-the-pearl-harbor-attack/japanese-aircraft-during-and-after-the-raid.html.

Jones, Heather, "Prisoners of War in 1914–1918." *International Encyclopedia of the First World War*. Ute Daniel, Peter Gatrell, Oliver Janz, Heather Jones, Jennifer Keene, Alan Kramer, and Bill Nasson, eds. Berlin: Freie Universität Berlin, 2014. DOI: 10.15463/ie1418.10475. https://encyclopedia.1914-1918-online.net/article/prisoners_of_war.

"Joseph K. Taussig Jr." *Wikipedia*. February 11, 2019. Accessed February 24, 2019. https://en.wikipedia.org/wiki/Joseph_K._Taussig_Jr.

Kaller, Brian. "Why We Need Superheroes." American Conservative. Accessed January 8, 2019. https://www.theamericanconservative.com/articles/why-we-need-superheroes/.

Kelly, William. "The Sortie of the USS *Nevada*." USS *Nevada* Sortie at Pearl Harbor. January 1, 1970. Accessed February 21, 2019. http://nevadasortieatpearlharbor.blogspot.com/.

Kilhefner, Johnny. "The Duties of a Boatswain." Chron.com. November 9, 2016. Accessed January 4, 2019. https://work.chron.com/duties-boatswain-20927.html.

Kopp, Jennifer Brownstone. "History, This Is Cape May, Congress Hall in 2002." CapeMay.com. June 1, 2002. https://www.capemay.com/blog/2002/06/congress-hall-in-2002/.

"Kuril Islands." *Wikipedia*. January 14, 2019. Accessed January 21, 2019. https://en.wikipedia.org/wiki/Kuril_Islands.

Landphair, Ted. "'War of 1812' Flag Still Inspires." VOA. September 10, 2012. Accessed March 2, 2019. https://www.voanews.com/a/war-of-1812-flag-still-inspires-after-200-years/1504894.html.

"The Legend behind Hawaii's Goddess of Fire." *Roberts Hawaii* (blog). Accessed April 21, 2019. https://www.robertshawaii.com/blog/legend-behind-hawaiis-goddess-fire/.

"List of United States Navy Ratings." *Wikipedia*. January 1, 2019. Accessed February 18, 2019. https://en.wikipedia.org/wiki/List_of_United_States_Navy_ratings.

Lockwood, Eric. "Navy Action Reports Tell the Story of Pearl Harbor Attack." *Sextant*, December 4, 2014. Accessed March 2, 2019. http://usnhistory.navylive.dodlive.mil/2014/12/04/navy-action-reports-tell-the-story-of-pearl-harbor-attack/.

Loproto, Mark. "Howard Linn, USS *Nevada* Survivor." Pearl Harbor Reservations. May 5, 2018. Accessed February 25, 2019. https://pearlharbor.org/howard-linn-uss-nevada-survivor/.

Lord, Walter. *Day of Infamy*. New York: Henry Holt and Company, 1957.

Mac, Mister. TheLeanSubmariner: Steel Boats, Iron Men, and Their Stories (Plus a Bit More). "The Patten Family and the USS *Nevada* (1941)." September 7, 2018.

"Manayunk, Philadelphia." *Wikipedia*. January 1, 2019. Accessed January 20, 2019. https://en.wikipedia.org/wiki/Manayunk,_Philadelphia.

Marcel, Rick, Rick, Rachana Chhin, Foxie, Joe, De Liliis, Regina Handin, Jo Waldron, Joie Munda, Don Bolognese, Shan Perera, Angela, and Polycarp. "Top 50 Saints' Quotes." Aggie Catholic Blog. May 16, 2018. Accessed February 18, 2019. https://www.aggiecatholicblog.org/2013/08/top-50-saints-quotes/.

Matson, Helen. "Dorwin Lamkin—Pearl Harbor Survivor." *Examiner of East Jackson County*, May 2, 2012. Accessed April 19, 2019. https://www.examiner.net/x1942569899/Dorwin-Lamkin-Pearl-Harbor-Survivor.

McCarthy, Jack. "Paper and Papermaking." *Encyclopedia of Greater Philadelphia*. Accessed January 7, 2019. https://philadelphiaencyclopedia.org/archive/paper-and-papermaking/.

McDermott, Annette. "How the Sinking of *Lusitania* Changed World War I." History.com. April 17, 2018. Accessed February 18, 2019. https://www.history.com/news/how-the-sinking-of-lusitania-changed-wwi.

McIntosh, Elizabeth P. "Honolulu after Pearl Harbor: A Report Published for the First Time, 71 Years Later." *Washington Post,* December 6, 2012. Accessed January 3, 2019. https://www.washingtonpost.com/opinions/honolulu-after-pearl-harbor-a-report-published-for-the-first-time-71-years-later/2012/12/06/e9029986-3d69-11e2-bca3-aadc9b7e29c5_story.html?noredirect=on&utm_term=.8271525f32ef.

Merriam-Webster Dictionary. https://www.merriam-webster.com/dictionary/dreadnought.

Michal. "The Path to Pearl Harbor." National WWII Museum. New Orleans. December 5, 2018. Accessed January 4, 2019. https://www.nationalww2museum.org/war/articles/path-pearl-harbor.

"Moment of Decision: PFC Elmer (Remle) Grayson, USMC, USS *Nevada.*" Crucibleteachnotes.html. 1999. Submitted by Vicki Grayson. Accessed February 25, 2019. http://www.ibiblio.org/phha/Elmer.html.

"Nakajima B5N." *Wikipedia.* September 16, 2018. Accessed February 25, 2019. https://en.wikipedia.org/wiki/Nakajima_B5N.

"Naval History and Heritage Command." Naval History and Heritage Command. Accessed January 3, 2019. https://www.history.navy.mil/research/histories/ship-histories/danfs/n/nevada-ii.html.

"Naval History and Heritage Command." Naval History and Heritage Command. Accessed February 25, 2019. https://www.history.navy.mil/

content/history/nhhc/research/library/online-reading-room/title-list-alphabetically/p/pearl-harbor-navy-medical-activities.html.

"Naval History and Heritage Command." Naval History and Heritage Command. September 21, 2015. Accessed January 28, 2019. https://www.history.navy.mil/content/history/nhhc/research/library/oral-histories/wwii/pearl-harbor/pearl-harbor-attack-lt-erickson.html.

"Naval History and Heritage Command." Naval History and Heritage Command. September 23, 2015. Accessed January 28, 2019. Captain Lacouture, USN. Oral History of the Pearl Harbor Attack, 7 December 1941. https://www.history.navy.mil/research/library/oral-histories/wwii/pearl-harbor/pearl-harbor-attack-captain-lacouture-uss-blue.html.

"Naval History and Heritage Command." Naval History and Heritage Command. February 21, 2018. Accessed January 5, 2019. https://www.history.navy.mil/content/history/nhhc/research/archives/digitized-collections/action-reports/wwii-pearl-harbor-attack/ships-m-r/uss-nevada-bb-36-action-report.html.

"Naval History and Heritage Command." National Museum of the Navy. https://www.history.navy.mil/content/history/nhhc/search.html?q=uss+saratoga.

NavSource Naval History Photographic History of the US Navy. "Battleship Photo Archive." http://navsource.org/archives/01/pdf/014801x.pdf.

NavySNAmedia. YouTube. June 5, 2014. Accessed January 27, 2019. https://www.youtube.com/watch?v=NnWUrK1GkUw&feature=youtu.be.

"Nebraska's Pearl Harbor Survivors Recount Their Memories of Dec. 7, 1941." Omaha.com. December 4, 2016. Accessed March 3, 2019. https://

www.omaha.com/news/military/nebraska-s-pearl-harbor-survivors-recount-their-memories-of-dec/article_74e23013-0467-5914-821e-63752338313a.html.

Nelson, Craig. *Pearl Harbor: From Infamy to Greatness*. London: Weidenfeld and Nicolson, 2018.

"NH 120956 Admiral Sir Rosslyn Wemyss, RN, 1st Sea Lord Inspecting Men on Board USS *Melville*." Naval History and Heritage Command. Accessed January 21, 2019. https://www.history.navy.mil/content/history/nhhc/our-collections/photography/numerical-list-of-images/nhhc-series/nh-series/NH-120000/NH-120956.html.

"NH 44472 USS *Panther* (AD-6)." Naval History and Heritage Command. Accessed January 21, 2019. https://www.history.navy.mil/content/history/nhhc/our-collections/photography/numerical-list-of-images/nhhc-series/nh-series/NH-44000/NH-44472.html.

"NH 46202 USS *Melville*." Naval History and Heritage Command. Accessed January 21, 2019. https://www.history.navy.mil/content/history/nhhc/research/publications/documentary-histories/wwi/september-1917/illustrations/crew-on-uss-melville.html.

"NH 46203 USS *Melville*." Naval History and Heritage Command. Accessed January 21, 2019. https://www.history.navy.mil/content/history/nhhc/our-collections/photography/numerical-list-of-images/nhhc-series/nh-series/NH-46000/NH-46203.html.

"NH 54515 USS *Dixie* (AD-1)." Naval History and Heritage Command. Accessed January 21, 2019. https://www.history.navy.mil/content/history/nhhc/our-collections/photography/numerical-list-of-images/nhhc-series/nh-series/NH-54000/NH-54515.html.

"NH 64306 USS *Nevada* (BB-36)." Naval History and Heritage Command. Accessed January 3, 2019. https://www.history.navy.mil/our-collections/photography/wars-and-events/world-war-ii/pearl-harbor-raid/battleship-row-during-the-pearl-harbor-attack/uss-nevada-during-the-pearl-harbor-attack/nh-64306-pearl-harbor-attack.html.

"NH 64306 USS *Nevada* (BB-36)." Naval History and Heritage Command. Accessed January 5, 2019. https://www.history.navy.mil/content/history/nhhc/our-collections/photography/wars-and-events/world-war-ii/pearl-harbor-raid/battleship-row-during-the-pearl-harbor-attack/uss-nevada-during-the-pearl-harbor-attack/nh-64306-pearl-harbor-attack.html.

"NH 64484 Pearl Harbor Attack, 7 December 1941." Naval History and Heritage Command. Accessed January 3, 2019. https://www.history.navy.mil/our-collections/photography/wars-and-events/world-war-ii/pearl-harbor-raid/battleship-row-during-the-pearl-harbor-attack/uss-nevada-during-the-pearl-harbor-attack/nh-64484-pearl-harbor-attack.html.

"NH 64484 Pearl Harbor Attack, 7 December 1941." Naval History and Heritage Command. Accessed January 5, 2019. https://www.history.navy.mil/content/history/nhhc/our-collections/photography/wars-and-events/world-war-ii/pearl-harbor-raid/battleship-row-during-the-pearl-harbor-attack/uss-nevada-during-the-pearl-harbor-attack/nh-64484-pearl-harbor-attack.html.

"NH 804 USS *Melville* (Destroyer Tender # 2)." Naval History and Heritage Command. Accessed January 7, 2019. https://www.history.navy.mil/content/history/nhhc/our-collections/photography/numerical-list-of-images/nhhc-series/nh-series/nh-1---nh-3067/nh-800---nh-899/nh-804-uss-melville--destroyer-tender---2-.html.

"NH 804 USS *Melville* (Destroyer Tender # 2)." Naval History and Heritage Command. Accessed January 21, 2019. https://www.history.navy.mil/content/history/nhhc/our-collections/photography/numerical-list-of-images/nhhc-series/nh-series/nh-1---nh-3067/nh-800---nh-899/nh-804-uss-melville--destroyer-tender---2-.html.

"NH 83108 Pearl Harbor Raid, 7 December 1941." Naval History and Heritage Command. Accessed January 3, 2019. https://www.history.navy.mil/our-collections/photography/wars-and-events/world-war-ii/pearl-harbor-raid/overall-views-of-the-pearl-harbor-attack/NH-83108.html.

"NH 83109 Pearl Harbor Raid, 7 December 1941." Naval History and Heritage Command. Accessed January 3, 2019. https://www.history.navy.mil/our-collections/photography/wars-and-events/world-war-ii/pearl-harbor-raid/overall-views-of-the-pearl-harbor-attack/NH-83109.html.

"NH 84 USS *Dixie* (AD-1), Destroyer Tender, 1898–1922." Naval History and Heritage Command. Accessed January 6, 2019. https://www.history.navy.mil/content/history/nhhc/our-collections/photography/numerical-list-of-images/nhhc-series/nh-series/NH-00001/NH-84.html.

"NH 84003 USS *Nevada* (BB-36)." Naval History and Heritage Command. Accessed January 3, 2019. https://www.history.navy.mil/our-collections/photography/wars-and-events/world-war-ii/pearl-harbor-raid/battleship-row-during-the-pearl-harbor-attack/uss-nevada-during-the-pearl-harbor-attack/nh-84003-pearl-harbor-attack.html.

"NH 84003 USS *Nevada* (BB-36)." Naval History and Heritage Command. Accessed January 5, 2019. https://www.history.navy.mil/content/history/nhhc/our-collections/photography/wars-and-events/world-war-ii/pearl-harbor-raid/battleship-row-during-the-pearl-harbor-attack/

uss-nevada-during-the-pearl-harbor-attack/nh-84003-pearl-harbor-attack.html.

"NH 91333 HA-19." Naval History and Heritage Command. Accessed January 8, 2019. https://www.history.navy.mil/content/history/nhhc/our-collections/photography/wars-and-events/world-war-ii/pearl-harbor-raid/japanese-forces-in-the-pearl-harbor-attack/japanese-midget-submarines-used-in-the-attack-on-pearl-harbor/NH-91333.html.

"NH 91333 HA-19." Naval History and Heritage Command. Accessed January 21, 2019. https://www.history.navy.mil/content/history/nhhc/our-collections/photography/wars-and-events/world-war-ii/pearl-harbor-raid/japanese-forces-in-the-pearl-harbor-attack/japanese-midget-submarines-used-in-the-attack-on-pearl-harbor/NH-91333.html.

"NH 94379 Pearl Harbor Attack, 7 December 1941." Naval History and Heritage Command. Accessed January 5, 2019. https://www.history.navy.mil/content/history/nhhc/our-collections/photography/wars-and-events/world-war-ii/pearl-harbor-raid/battleship-row-during-the-pearl-harbor-attack/uss-west-virginia-and-uss-tennessee-during-the-pearl-harbor-atta/NH-94379.html.

"NH 97376 Pearl Harbor Attack, 7 December 1941." Naval History and Heritage Command. Accessed January 3, 2019. https://www.history.navy.mil/our-collections/photography/wars-and-events/world-war-ii/pearl-harbor-raid/overall-views-of-the-pearl-harbor-attack/NH-97376.html.

"NH 97378 Pearl Harbor Attack, 7 December 1941." Naval History and Heritage Command. Accessed January 5, 2019. https://www.history.navy.mil/our-collections/photography/wars-and-events/world-war-ii/

pearl-harbor-raid/battleship-row-during-the-pearl-harbor-attack/general-views/NH-97378.html.

"NH 97379 Pearl Harbor Attack, 7 December 1941." Naval History and Heritage Command. Accessed January 5, 2019. https://www.history.navy.mil/content/history/nhhc/our-collections/photography/wars-and-events/world-war-ii/pearl-harbor-raid/battleship-row-during-the-pearl-harbor-attack/uss-arizona-during-the-pearl-harbor-attack/NH-97379.html.

"NH 97380 Pearl Harbor Attack, 7 December 1941." Naval History and Heritage Command. Accessed January 5, 2019. https://www.history.navy.mil/content/history/nhhc/our-collections/photography/wars-and-events/world-war-ii/pearl-harbor-raid/battleship-row-during-the-pearl-harbor-attack/uss-arizona-during-the-pearl-harbor-attack/NH-97380.html.

"NH 97396 Pearl Harbor Attack, 7 December 1941." Naval History and Heritage Command. Accessed January 3, 2019. https://www.history.navy.mil/our-collections/photography/wars-and-events/world-war-ii/pearl-harbor-raid/battleship-row-during-the-pearl-harbor-attack/uss-nevada-during-the-pearl-harbor-attack/NH-97396.html.

"NH 97396 Pearl Harbor Attack, 7 December 1941." Naval History and Heritage Command. Accessed January 5, 2019. https://www.history.navy.mil/content/history/nhhc/our-collections/photography/wars-and-events/world-war-ii/pearl-harbor-raid/battleship-row-during-the-pearl-harbor-attack/uss-nevada-during-the-pearl-harbor-attack/NH-97396.html.

"NH 97397 Pearl Harbor Attack, 7 December 1941." Naval History and Heritage Command. Accessed January 3, 2019. https://www.history.navy.mil/our-collections/photography/wars-and-events/world-war-ii/

pearl-harbor-raid/battleship-row-during-the-pearl-harbor-attack/uss-nevada-during-the-pearl-harbor-attack/NH-97397.html.

"NH 97397 Pearl Harbor Attack, 7 December 1941." Naval History and Heritage Command. Accessed January 5, 2019. https://www.history.navy.mil/content/history/nhhc/our-collections/photography/wars-and-events/world-war-ii/pearl-harbor-raid/battleship-row-during-the-pearl-harbor-attack/uss-nevada-during-the-pearl-harbor-attack/NH-97397.html.

"NHHC." Naval History and Heritage Command. Accessed January 22, 2019. https://www.history.navy.mil/.

Otte, Maarten. *The American Expeditionary Forces in the Great War Meuse-Argonne Montfaucon*. South Yorkshire: Pen and Sword Military, 2018.

"Our Lady Star of the Sea Chaplet Prayer." RosaryAndChaplets.Com: Seven Sorrows Seven Dolors of Mary Servite Rosary Chaplet, Prayer. Accessed January 21, 2019. http://www.rosaryandchaplets.com/chaplets/our_lady_star_sea_prayer.html.

"Overall Views of the Pearl Harbor Attack." Naval History and Heritage Command. Accessed January 3, 2019. https://www.history.navy.mil/our-collections/photography/wars-and-events/world-war-ii/pearl-harbor-raid/overall-views-of-the-pearl-harbor-attack.html.

Panko, Ray. "The *Nevada*'s Run." Pearl Harbor Aviation Museum. June 1, 2018. Accessed February 18, 2019. https://www.pearlharboraviationmuseum.org/pearl-harbor-blog/the-nevadas-run/.

"Pearl Harbor Attack." *Encyclopædia Britannica*. December 17, 2018. Accessed January 8, 2019. https://www.britannica.com/event/Pearl-Harbor-attack.

"Pearl Harbor Attack." Naval History and Heritage Command. Accessed January 2, 2019. https://www.history.navy.mil/browse-by-topic/wars-conflicts-and-operations/world-war-ii/1941/pearl-harbor.html.

"Pearl Harbor in Hawaii." USS *Tennessee* Battleship. PearlHarborinHawaii.com. Accessed February 20, 2019. https://www.pearlharborinhawaii.com/ussnevada.html.

"Pearl Harbor Hero Chief Boatswain Edwin Hill." Visit Pearl Harbor. April 12, 2018. Accessed January 3, 2019. https://visitpearlharbor.org/pearl-harbor-hero-edwin-hill/.

"Pearl Harbor Historic Sites." About Pearl Harbor. 2016. Accessed April 20, 2019. http://www.pearlharborhistoricsites.org/pearl-harbor/.

"Pearl Harbor in 1940–1941." Naval History and Heritage Command. Accessed January 4, 2019. https://www.history.navy.mil/our-collections/photography/wars-and-events/world-war-ii/pearl-harbor-raid/pearl-harbor-in-1940-1941.html.

"Pearl Harbor Infographic." Naval History and Heritage Command. Accessed January 2, 2019. https://w ww.history.navy.mil/news-and-events/multimedia-gallery/infographics/history/pearl-harbor-infographic.html.

"Pearl Harbor Memorial." City of Forks City Limit Sign (Forks, Washington). April 13, 2017. Stock footage video 28374238. Shutterstock. Accessed January 4, 2019. https://www.shutterstock.com/

download/confirm/244397059?src=kdJXZo_9af7CRHBCyc0zGg-1-47&size=medium_jpg.

"Pearl Harbor Navy Medical Activities." Crucibleteachnotes.html. Administrative History Section, Administrative Division, Bureau of Medicine and Surgery. "The United States Navy Medical Department at War, 1941–1945" 1, parts 1–2 (1946): 1–31. This manuscript, identified as United States Naval Administrative History of World War II #68-A, is located in Navy Department Library's Rare Book Room. Transcribed and formatted by Patrick Clancey. Accessed February 24, 2019. https://www.ibiblio.org/hyperwar/USN/rep/Pearl/Medical.html.

"Pearl Harbor Raid." Naval History and Heritage Command. Accessed January 3, 2019. https://www.history.navy.mil/our-collections/photography/wars-and-events/world-war-ii/pearl-harbor-raid.html.

Pennsylvania Military Museum. "USS *Pennsylvania* (BB-38)." Pennsylvania Historical and Museum Commission. https://www.pamilmuseum.org/uss-pennsylvania.

"Pennsylvania, WWI Veterans Service and Compensation Files, 1917–1919, 1934–1948 for Edwin Joseph Hill." Ancestry.com.

Perry, Mark J. "Lieutenant Survives the Pearl Harbor Attack aboard the USS *Nevada*." December 7, 2018. Originally appeared in *World War II* (January 1998). Accessed February 20, 2019. https://www.historynet.com/pearl-harbor-attack-lieutenant-lawrence-ruff-survived-attack-aboard-uss-nevada.htm.

Prange, Gordon W., Donald M. Goldstein, and Katherine V. Dillon. *At Dawn We Slept: The Untold Story of Pearl Harbor*. New York: Penguin, 1991.

"Prelude to War: Japanese Strike Force Takes Aim at Pearl Harbor." *Sextant*. AccessedJanuary21,2019.http://usnhistory.navylive.dodlive.mil/2014/11/26/prelude-to-war-japanese-strike-force-takes-aim-at-pearl-harbor/.

Projects, Contributors to Wikimedia. "County Seat City in Philadelphia County, Pennsylvania; Sixth Largest City in the United States by Population." Wikimedia Commons. December 12, 2018. Accessed January 9, 2019. https://commons.wikimedia.org/wiki/Philadelphia#/media/File:Aerial_view_of_Philadelphia.jpg.

Projects, Contributors to Wikimedia. "County Seat City in Philadelphia County, Pennsylvania; Sixth Largest City in the United States by Population." Wikimedia Commons. December 12, 2018. Accessed January 21, 2019. https://commons.wikimedia.org/wiki/Philadelphia#/media/File:FDR_accepts_the_nomination_for_the_Presidency_in_speech_at_Franklin_Field,_Philadelphia,_PA._June_27,_1936.jpg.

Quintiliani, Patricia S. "Our Lady Star of the Sea Chaplet Prayer." November 2008. Accessed January 9, 2019. http://www.rosaryandchaplets.com/chaplets/our_lady_star_sea_prayer.html.

Reports, Tribune Wire. "Pearl Harbor Survivor, 92, from Geneva Visits USS *Nevada* Exhibit." *Chicago Tribune*, October 17, 2015. Accessed February 28, 2019. https://www.chicagotribune.com/suburbs/batavia-geneva-st-charles/ct-pearl-harbor-survivor-geneva-20151017-story.html.

Revolvy LLC. "'Edwin J. Hill' on Revolvy.com." Trivia Quizzes. Accessed January 3, 2019. https://www.revolvy.com/page/Edwin-J.-Hill.

Richards, Stu. "Schuylkill County at Pearl Harbor December 7, 1941." Schuylkill County Pennsylvania Military History. January 1, 1970. Accessed February 25, 2019. http://schuylkillcountymilitaryhistory.blogspot.com/2012/12/schuylkill-county-at-pearl-harbor.html.

Robbins, Don. "USS *Nevada* Survivor Is Honored at Wayside Exhibit Unveiling." *Ho'okele News*, December 15, 2012. http://www.hookelenews.com/uss-nevada-survivor-is-honored-at-wayside-exhibit-unveiling/.

Rodgers, J. David. "How One Man Can Change History: An Example of Diligence." Reassessment of the St. Francis Dam Failure. May 31, 2013. Accessed February 20, 2019. https://web.mst.edu/~rogersda/american&military_history/Rogers-HowOneManCanChangeHistory-Minimum-May31-2013.pdf.

Rogers, Keith. "Handful of USS *Nevada* Shipmates Reunite in Las Vegas." *Las Vegas Review-Journal*, February 18, 2017. Accessed February 28, 2019. https://www.reviewjournal.com/news/military/handful-of-uss-nevada-shipmates-reunite-in-las-vegas/.

Rogers, Keith. "Remembering the USS *Nevada*'s Daring Run for the Sea during Attack on Pearl Harbor." *Las Vegas Review-Journal*, February 19, 2017. Accessed January 3, 2019. https://www.reviewjournal.com/news/military/remembering-the-uss-nevadas-daring-run-for-the-sea-during-attack-on-pearl-harbor/.

Rogers, Keith. "USS *Nevada* and Her Crew Honored Anew for Pearl Harbor Exploits." *Las Vegas-Review Journal*, December 9, 2016. Accessed February 27, 2019. https://www.reviewjournal.com/news/military/uss-nevada-and-her-crew-honored-anew-for-pearl-harbor-exploits/.

Ross, Donald K., and Helen L. *0755 the Heroes of Pearl Harbor.* Port Orchard, WA: Rokalu Press, 1988.

Ross, Donald K., and Helen L. *Men of Valor.* Burley, Washington: Coffee Break Press, 1980.

"Roxborough, Philadelphia." *Wikipedia.* January 5, 2019. Accessed January 19, 2019. https://en.wikipedia.org/wiki/Roxborough,_Philadelphia.

"Sailors as Infantry in the US Navy." Naval History and Heritage Command. Accessed January 26, 2019. https://www.history.navy.mil/research/library/online-reading-room/title-list-alphabetically/s/sailors-as-infantry-us-navy.html#early.

Salute Uniforms. "U.S. Navy Boatswain's Mate (BM) Rating Badge." http://www.uniforms-4u.com/p-navy-dress-blue-uniform-rating-badge-bm-1st-class-po-male-red-. http://www.Ancestry.comchevrons-3930.aspx.

Scarpaci, Wayne. *Battleship Nevada: The Extraordinary Ship of Firsts.* 3rd ed. Gardnerville, NV: Art by Wayne, 2014.

"Scrip." *Wikipedia.* December 5, 2018. Accessed January 8, 2019. https://en.wikipedia.org/wiki/Scrip.

"Search." Naval History and Heritage Command. Accessed April 15, 2019. https://www.history.navy.mil/content/history/nhhc/search.html?q=uss saratoga.

Sehe, Charles. "Nevada Appeal." *Lahontan Valley News*, November 10, 2015. https://www.nevadaappeal.com/news/opinion/remembering-pearl-harbor-uss-nevada-a-spirited-ship/#.

Sehe, Charles T. "I Served on the Battleship *Nevada* (and Survived Pearl Harbor)." *The National Interest* (blog). September 1, 2018. Accessed February 28, 2019. Originally published in 2017. This article by Charles T. Sehe originally appeared on the Warfare History Network. https://nationalinterest.org/blog/buzz/i-served-battleship-nevada-and-survived-pearl-harbor-30282?page=0,5.

Sehe, Charles, Brad Coman, Arica Davis, Nevada Appeal, Nevada Appeal, US Navy, and AP. US War Department. "Remembering Pearl Harbor: USS *Nevada* 'A Spirited Ship.'" Nevada Appeal. December 7, 2016. Accessed February 24, 2019. Charles Sehe, a Minnesota resident, is a Pearl Harbor attack survivor. Sehe was aboard the USS *Nevada* during the attack. https://www.nevadaappeal.com/news/opinion/remembering-pearl-harbor-uss-nevada-a-spirited-ship/#.

"Shadow Box." Navy USS *Onward* (1852) Clipper Ship. Navy Veteran Locator. Accessed January 28, 2019. https://navy.togetherweserved.com/usn/servlet/tws.webapp.WebApp?cmd=ShadowBoxProfile&type=Person&ID=225895.

"Shadow Box." TogetherWeServed. Accessed August 20, 2019. https://marines.togetherweserved.com/usmc/servlet/tws.webapp.WebApp?cmd=ShadowBoxProfile&type=Person&ID=180380.

Shakes, Willy. "December 7, 1941: Attack on Pearl Harbor." History 101. December 8, 2018. Accessed January 8, 2019. http://www.history101.com/december-7-1941-attack-pearl-harbor/.

Shell Shock: The Psychological Scars of World War 1: The Great War Special. April 18, 2016. Accessed January 25, 2019. The Great War series. https://www.youtube.com/watch?v=kvTRJZGWqF8.

Sherman, Stephen. "USS *Nevada* (BB-36): Her Last Flight and Disappearance." June 2007. Updated March 21, 2012. Accessed February 20, 2019. http://acepilots.com/ships/nevada.html.

Silverstone, Paul. "A New Generation of Dreadnoughts." *Sea Classics* (August 1989).

"Sixty Native American Quotes, Sayings and Wisdom." Inspiring Pictures Quotes. SayingImages.com. September 14, 2017. Accessed February 18, 2019. https://sayingimages.com/native-american-quotes/.

Slackman, Michael. *Remembering Pearl Harbor: The Story of the USS* Arizona *Memorial.* Honolulu, Hawaii: Arizona Memorial Museum Association, 1990.

"Slinky." *Wikipedia.* January 6, 2019. Accessed January 20, 2019. https://en.wikipedia.org/wiki/Slinky.

Smitha, Frank E. "The Attack at Pearl Harbor and the Philippines." 2014. Accessed March 15, 2019. http://www.fsmitha.com/h2/ch22b4.htm.

Sobocinski, Andre B. "Navy Medicine at Pearl Harbor (Dec. 7, 1941)." Navy Medicine. Accessed February 24, 2019. http://navymedicine.navylive.dodlive.mil/archives/3809.

"Some Jewish Quotes/Sayings for 9/11 Yahrtzeit." Bay Area Jewish Healing Center. Accessed February 18, 2019. https://jewishhealingcenter.org/resources/disaster-response/some-jewish-quotessayings-for-911-yahrtzeit/.

"St. John the Baptist Roman Catholic Church, Manayunk." *Wikipedia*. February 19, 2018. Accessed January 20, 2019. https://en.wikipedia.org/wiki/St._John_the_Baptist_Roman_Catholic_Church,_Manayunk.

"St. John the Baptist." Philadelphia Church Project. Accessed January 9, 2019. http://www.phillychurchproject.com/st-john-the-baptist/.

Staff. "December 7, 1941: Attack on Pearl Harbor." History 101. December 8, 2018. Accessed January 21, 2019. http://www.history101.com/december-7-1941-attack-pearl-harbor/.

Staff, USO. "The USO at Pearl Harbor, 77 Years Later." United Service Organizations. 2019. Accessed February 24, 2019. https://www.uso.org/stories/1938-the-uso-at-pearl-harbor-76-years-later.

"Star-Spangled Banner (flag)." *Wikipedia*. January 14, 2019. Accessed March 2, 2019. https://en.wikipedia.org/wiki/Star-Spangled_Banner_(flag).

Stewart, Chad. "9 Things You Might Not Know about the Attack on Pearl Harbor." United Service Organizations. 2019. Accessed February 24, 2019. https://www.uso.org/stories/1732-9-things-you-might-not-know-about-the-attack-on-pearl-harbor.

"Stories of Valor on a Day of Infamy." *Sextant*. Accessed January 4, 2019. http://usnhistory.navylive.dodlive.mil/2016/12/05/stories-of-valor-on-a-day-of-infamy/.

Stratton, Donald, and Ken Gire. *All the Gallant Men: The First Memoir by a USS* Arizona *Survivor*. New York: HarperCollins, 2016.

Sulivan, Taira. "The Sinking of the USS *Nevada* (BB 36)." Naval History Blog. US Naval Institute. December 6, 2018. https://www.navalhistory.org/2018/12/06/the-sinking-of-the-uss-nevada-bb-36.

"A Sunday in December: Chapter 3: Hell in the Harbor." *Los Angeles Times*, December 3, 1991. Accessed February 25, 2019. http://articles.latimes.com/1991-12-03/news/wr-737_1_pearl-harbor/5.

Sybil Ludington. Statue in Carmel, New York. Statues of Historic Figures on Waymarking.com. Accessed January 8, 2019. http://www.waymarking.com/gallery/image.aspx?f=1&guid=72d7cd9e-ab33-4de1-bfa1-92f85fcfe858.

Sybil Ludington. Statue in Carmel, New York. Statues of Historic Figures on Waymarking.com. Accessed January 27, 2019. http://www.waymarking.com/waymarks/WMPZD5_Rear_Admiral_Herman_J_Kossler_Monument_Mount_Pleasant_SC.

Taussig, Lieutenant J. K. "My Crew at Pearl Harbor." *Coronet* 13, no 6. (April 1943): 137–149.

"The Tenth Oldest Parish in the Archdiocese of Philadelphia." Accessed January 20, 2019. http://www.stjohnmanayunk.org/.

Thompson, Ben. "Badass of the Week: Ching Shih." Accessed January 3, 2019. http://www.badassoftheweek.com/edwinhill.html.

Tischler, Susan. "A Look at Early Victorian Architecture." CapeMay.com. September 1, 2006. https://www.capemay.com/blog/2006/09/a-look-at-early-victorian-architecture/.

Tischler, Susan. "Cape May on Fire." CapeMay.com. November 1, 2003. https://www.capemay.com/blog/2003/11/cape-may-on-fire/.

"Treaty of Shackamaxon." *Encyclopedia of Greater Philadelphia*. Accessed January 20, 2019. https://philadelphiaencyclopedia.org/archive/paper-and-papermaking/.

"Type 91 Torpedo." *Wikipedia*. October 11, 2018. Accessed February 24, 2019. https://en.wikipedia.org/wiki/Type_91_torpedo.

"Uniforms of the US Navy 1942–1943." Naval History and Heritage Command. Accessed January 7, 2019. https://www.history.navy.mil/content/history/nhhc/browse-by-topic/heritage/uniforms-and-personal-equipment/uniforms-1942-1943.html.

US Naval Archives and Getty Images. iStockphoto. "USS *Nevada* Fought Heroically at Pearl Harbor." Nevada Appeal. December 6, 2016. Accessed February 20, 2019. https://www.nevadaappeal.com/news/lahontan-valley/uss-nevada-fought-heroically-at-pearl-harbor/.

"US Navy Boatswain's Mate (BM) Rating Badge." The Crackerjack: The History of the Navy's Enlisted Dress Uniform. Accessed February 27, 2019. http://www.uniforms-4u.com/p-navy-dress-blue-uniform-rating-badge-bm-1st-class-po-male-red-chevrons-3930.aspx.

"US Navy Boatswain's Mate (BM) Rating Badge." US Military Uniforms and Insignia Manufacturer: The Salute Uniforms. Accessed April 13, 2019. http://www.uniforms-4u.com/p-navy-dress-blue-uniform-rating-badge-bm-1st-class-po-male-red-chevrons-3930.aspx.

"US Navy Chief Warrant Officer 5 Coat Rank Device." US Military Uniforms and Insignia Manufacturer: The Salute Uniforms. Accessed April 13, 2019. http://www.uniforms-4u.com/p-us-navy-coat-device-warrant-officer-5-6559.aspx.

"USNavySailorEdwinJ.Hill'sInsaneActofBraveryduringtheAttackonPearl Harbor." *VintageNews*, April11,2017. AccessedJanuary21,2019. https://www.thevintagenews.com/2017/04/11/us-navy-sailor-edwin-j-hills-insane-act-of-bravery-during-the-attack-on-pearl-harbor/?fbclid=IwAR3hp6eQrot2ccVu0osvA-vHyw4BPVs6AvMZqyAhIqfTwaZURV33tHGN7kk.

US Navy. "Silent Professionals: History of the Rank of Chief Petty Officer." Navy Live. Accessed April 13, 2019. https://navylive.dodlive.mil/2015/03/31/happy-122nd-birthday-chief-petty-officers/.

"US, World War I Draft Registration Cards, 1917–1918 for Edward J Hill." Ancestry. Accessed January 7, 2019. https://www.ancestry.com/interactive/6482/005270414_03716/25280914?backurl=https://www.ancestry.com/family-tree/person/tree/157261159/person/172068322022/facts/citation/642091986190/edit/record.

"USNHistory.Navylive.Dolive.Mil." *Sextant*. Navy History Matters. January 1, 1970. https://usnhistory.navylive.dodlive.mil/2014/11/26/prelude-to-war-japanese-strike-force-takes-aim-at-pearl-harbor/.

"USS *Arizona* (BB-39)." Naval History and Heritage Command. Accessed January 2, 2019. https://www.history.navy.mil/research/underwater-archaeology/sites-and-projects/ship-wrecksites/uss-arizona-bb-39.html.

"USS *Dixie* (1893)." *Wikipedia*. July 14, 2018. Accessed January 6, 2019. https://en.wikipedia.org/wiki/USS_Dixie_(1893).

"USS *Hill* (DE-141)." *Wikipedia*. October 21, 2017. Accessed February 26, 2019. https://en.wikipedia.org/wiki/USS_Hill_(DE-141).

"USS *Melville* (AD-2)." *Wikipedia*. February 25, 2018. Accessed January 21, 2019. https://en.wikipedia.org/wiki/USS_Melville_(AD-2).

"USS *Melville*." USS *Shreveport* (LPD-12) Deployments and History. Accessed January 7, 2019. https://www.hullnumber.com/AD-2.

"USS *Nevada* (BB-36) Commemoration." Naval History and Heritage Command. November 8, 2017. Accessed February 24, 2019. https://www.history.navy.mil/content/history/nhhc/about-us/leadership/director/nevada.html.

"USS *Nevada* Pearl Harbor." Cell Code. Accessed January 9, 2019. https://cellcode.us/quotes/uss-nevada-pearl-harbor.html.

"USS *Nevada*: The Navy's First Super-Dreadnought." Visit Pearl Harbor. April 12, 2018. Accessed February 25, 2019. https://visitpearlharbor.org/uss-nevada-navys-first-super-dreadnought/.

"USS *Nevada* during the Pearl Harbor Attack." Naval History and Heritage Command. Accessed January 3, 2019. https://www.history.navy.mil/our-collections/photography/wars-and-events/world-war-ii/pearl-harbor-raid/battleship-row-during-the-pearl-harbor-attack/uss-nevada-during-the-pearl-harbor-attack.html.

"USS *Nevada* during the Pearl Harbor Attack." Naval History and Heritage Command. Accessed January 5, 2019. https://www.history.navy.mil/content/history/nhhc/our-collections/photography/wars-and-events/world-war-ii/pearl-harbor-raid/battleship-row-during-the-pearl-harbor-attack/uss-nevada-during-the-pearl-harbor-attack.html.

"USS *Nevada* during the Pearl Harbor Attack." Naval History and Heritage Command. Accessed January 28, 2019. https://www.history.navy.mil/content/history/nhhc/our-collections/photography/wars-and-events/world-war-ii/pearl-harbor-raid/battleship-row-during-the-pearl-harbor-attack/uss-nevada-during-the-pearl-harbor-attack.html.

"USS *Panther* (1889)." *Wikipedia*. October 9, 2018. Accessed January 26, 2019. https://en.wikipedia.org/wiki/USS_Panther_(1889).

"USS *Pennsylvania*." Pennsylvania Military Museum. Accessed April 15, 2019. https://www.pamilmuseum.org/uss-pennsylvania.

"USS *Pennsylvania* (BB-38)." *Wikipedia*. February 8, 2019. Accessed February 22, 2019. https://en.wikipedia.org/wiki/USS_Pennsylvania_(BB-38).

"USS *Saratoga*." *Wikipedia*. https://en.wikipedia.org/wiki/USS_Saratoga_(CV-3).

UTB. "Donald K. Ross Medal of Honor Citation." Unto the Breach. October 30, 2018. Accessed April 4, 2019. http://www.victoryinstitute.net/blogs/utb/1941/12/07/donald-k-ross-medal-of-honor-citation/.

UTB. "Edwin J. Hill Medal of Honor Citation." Unto the Breach. October 30, 2018. Accessed January 3, 2019. http://www.victoryinstitute.net/blogs/utb/1941/12/07/edwin-j-hill-medal-of-honor-citation/.

Vachon, Duane A. "A Hero from Pennsylvania? Chief Boatswain Edwin Joseph Hill, USN (1894–1941)." *Hawaii Reporter*, November 15, 2010. Accessed January 3, 2019. http://www.hawaiireporter.com/a-hero-from-pennsylvania-chief-boatswain-edwin-joseph-hill-usn-1894-1941/.

Valdez, Maria G. "Flag Day Quotes: 10 Sayings to Celebrate Adoption of Star Spangled Banner." *Latin Times*, June 12, 2015. https://www.latintimes.com/flag-day-quotes-10-sayings-celebrate-adoption-star-spangled-banner-322307.

Verburg, Steven. "Veterans' Memories of Pearl Harbor Attack Still Sting 70 Years Later." *Wisconsin State Journal* (December 7, 2011).

Accessed February 26, 2019. https://madison.com/wsj/news/local/veterans-memories-of-pearl-harbor-attack-still-sting-years-later/article_5122404a-206d-11e1-ac38-0019bb2963f4.html.

"Victor Talking Machine Company." *Wikipedia*. January 23, 2019. Accessed January 27, 2019. https://en.wikipedia.org/wiki/Victor_Talking_Machine_Company.

"Wai Momi: Pearl Harbor through History." Visit Pearl Harbor. June 20, 2017. Accessed April 20, 2019. https://visitpearlharbor.org/pearl-harbor-through-history-part-1/.

"Warrant Officer (United States)." *Wikipedia*. February 20, 2019. Accessed February 22, 2019. https://en.wikipedia.org/wiki/Warrant_officer_(United_States).

Watson, Walter E. "Irish (The) and Ireland." *Encyclopedia of Greater Philadelphia*. Accessed January 20, 2019. https://philadelphiaencyclopedia.org/archive/irish-the-and-ireland/.

Webb, Pennylynn. "At 96, Pearl Harbor Vet Is Still a Survivor." *Palestine Herald*, July 26, 2017. Accessed February 28, 2019. https://www.palestineherald.com/community/at-pearl-harbor-vet-is-still-a-survivor/article_3414939a-71a2-11e7-aa3b-fb52d8f71c1c.html.

Webmaster. MMCM (SS) Greg Peterman, USN Ret. 2020. Goatlocker.org.

"Welcome to the Goatlocker." Site creator Greg Peterman, USN Ret. 1993. Accessed April 13, 2019. http://goatlocker.org/.

"William R. Furlong." *Wikipedia*. November 9, 2018. Accessed March 15, 2019. https://en.wikipedia.org/wiki/William_R._Furlong.

"William S. Pye." *Wikipedia*. March 29, 2019. Accessed April 9, 2019. https://en.wikipedia.org/wiki/William_S._Pye.

"World War I." Naval History and Heritage Command. Accessed January 26, 2019. https://www.history.navy.mil/browse-by-topic/wars-conflicts-and-operations/world-war-i.html.

"World War I Prisoners of War in Germany." *Wikipedia*. December 14, 2018. Accessed January 25, 2019. https://en.wikipedia.org/wiki/World_War_I_prisoners_of_war_in_Germany.

"World War I at Sea: United States Navy—Officer Ranks and Enlisted Rates." Accessed February 9, 2019. http://www.naval-history.net/WW1NavyUS-Ranks.htm.

Wright, Jim. "Don't Just Embrace the Crazy, Sidle Up Next to It and Lick Its Ear." Stonekettle Station. December 7, 2007. Accessed February 25, 2019. http://www.stonekettle.com/2007/12/remembering-december-7th.html.

"WWI Veterans Service and Compensation Files." Ancestry. Accessed January 26, 2019. https://www.ancestry.com/interactive/60884/41744_2421406272_1136-00421/1664291?backurl=https://www.ancestry.com/family-tree/person/tree/157899976/person/422071331243/facts/citation/1142098429535/edit/record.

"WWII USS Battleship *Nevada*." Pearl Harbor Visitors Bureau. Accessed February 24, 2019. https://visitpearlharbor.org/world-war-ii-battleships/uss-battleship-nevada/.

Yarnell, Paul R. "Navsource Online: Destroyer Escort Photo Archive." Submarine Photo Index. October 14, 2013. Created by Mike Smolinski. Accessed February 26, 2019. http://www.navsource.org/archives/06/141.htm.

Printed in the United States
by Baker & Taylor Publisher Services